WORLD CHANGER

World Changer

A Mother's Story

The Unbreakable Spirit of US Navy SEAL Aaron Vaughn

by
Karen Vaughn

Printed in the United States of America
26 25 24 23 22 21 20 19 18 17   1 2 3 4 5

ISBN-13 (paperback): 978-0-692-08774-9
ISBN-13 (hardcover): 978-1-943496-12-9

Library of Congress Control Number: 2017936659

Editor: Kara Starcher

Dedication

*This book is dedicated to Special Operations Chiefs
Aaron Vaughn and Brad Cavner, US Navy SEALs
Brothers in life. Brothers in death.*

*May all who walk in the freedom you provided
live lives worthy of your great sacrifice.
And to those still in the battle…*

Long Live the Brotherhood.

Aaron (far left) and Brad (far right)

Table of Contents

Foreword by Sean Hannity..ix

Introduction by Tracy Bowen..xi

A Special Note to Moms by Karen Vaughn xv

Part One: The Forging

Chapter 1   A Rocky Start..3

Chapter 2   The Battle of Becoming 9

Chapter 3   Childhood Joys..15

Chapter 4   Realities of Life..23

Chapter 5   The World around Him.................................... 27

Chapter 6   The Heart of a Teenager 35

Chapter 7   New Places, New Faces..................................... 41

Chapter 8   Broken Heart, Broken Dreams 49

Chapter 9   That Fateful Day 55

Part Two: The Warrior

Chapter 10   BUD/S Class 248 67

Chapter 11   A Creed to Live By 77

Chapter 12   A Stroke of Love Called You......................... 85

Chapter 13   The Big Day 91

Chapter 14   All in God's Plan 95

Chapter 15   Life as a SEAL...99

Chapter 16   God Is Good 107

Chapter 17   I'll See You in November 113

Chapter 18   August Sixth...121

Chapter 19   But God Was There 131

Chapter 20   How Great Thou Art 139

Chapter 21   Memorials and Tears 143

Part Three: The Legacy

Chapter 22   A Legacy of Love 157

Chapter 23   A World Redefined 163

Epilogue   The Legacy of a Life Well Lived 167

Study Guide

Introduction 177
The Word Is "No" 181
Discipline 183
Don't Spock It Up 185
Love Well, Live Well 189
Building Your Tribe 191
The Value System 193
Fear 195
The Fixer 199
Shelter Free Zone 201
Our Response 203
Resilience 205
Family Decisions 207
Be a Champion 209
The Winner's Circle 211
Work Ethic 213
Letting Go 215
Filling a New Role 217
Celebrate Life 219
When Danger Lurks 221
Freedom Is Not Free 223
Acknowledgments 229
About the Author 231

Foreword

by Sean Hannity

I'VE BEEN WORKING IN RADIO and television for over thirty years, and few stories have impacted me like the August 6, 2011, shoot down of the chopper Extortion 17 which killed thirty American troops, most of whom were members of the elite SEAL Team VI.

In the months following that tragic loss of life, I came to know Billy and Karen Vaughn as they publicly and privately searched for answers to the many questions surrounding that fateful event which claimed the life of their only son.

I remember the admiration I felt after the first time I interviewed them. Billy and Karen had suffered the unthinkable, and instead of being crippled by their sorrow, they used their pain to change people's lives and advocate for our nation. Over the past six years, I've watched them emerge on the national scene as powerful spokespeople for the principles and values that make America strong and safe.

Billy and Karen exposed and drew national attention to the Rules of Engagement imposed on the men and women still fighting overseas. They realized this battle wouldn't bring their son back, but they hoped their efforts would spare other parents the agony they had been forced to endure. They started fighting for VA reform so veterans could have access to the medical care they deserved when they came home from battle. Along with their daughter Tara the Vaughns built Operation 300, a nonprofit organization that holds adventure camps and mentor programs for children who've lost a father in service to our country.

Karen left the comfort of her home and hit the road on a national tour designed to encourage Americans to love their country enough to engage in the political process of keeping it healthy and strong. She's writing classroom curriculum to help American children understand the sacrifices made that have offered them the freedoms they enjoy. She also works with another nonprofit that educates, inspires, and encourages Americans to give back to those veterans who've given so much for us.

But, of course, that's not the end of her story.

Karen is now throwing her heart straight into the homes of every parent across this nation with this new book about raising her son, Aaron, into a man whose life and death quite literally changed thousands of lives, including my own. She takes you on a beautiful journey of watching him grow in courage, in grit, in patriotism, and in love. By the end of this book, you will feel like you've been a part of her family since their early days on a small farm in Northwest Tennessee.

You will mourn with Karen as she describes the weeks leading up to Aaron's final deployment and those hours after learning of his death, but at the same time, you'll find yourself inspired by the Vaughn's unwavering faith during some of the darkest times in their lives.

This book conveys a powerful message about a mother's love for her son and channels a sense of patriotism and love for country that is so desperately needed right now. As a father, it reinforces how I want to ensure my own children understand how rich their lives are because of the sacrifices of great men like Aaron...and great moms, like Karen.

Introduction

by Tracy Bowen

*In 2012, Karen received the following from a stranger
who would later become a dear friend.*

RED, WHITE, AND BLUE RUNS through my veins. I am a born and
bred small town girl from the mountains of South Carolina, and I
don't mean to suggest that Southerners are the only citizens who are truly
patriotic, but we do have our own unique version of love of the moth-
erland. We are in your face about it. From the way we talk about our
country in everyday conversation to the way that we have no problem
with quickly and no-holds-barred confronting anyone who would dare
demean America. From the large American flags that fly proudly in the
back of our pickup trucks to the full-scale celebrations of our national
holidays. In the South, the Fourth of July is as big as Christmas. Shoot, it
might be bigger. The carnival doesn't come to town at Christmas.

All the men in my family have been in the military. My Grandpa
Hobelman fought in World War II and my brother, Greg, has had the
pleasure of an all-expense paid trip to Afghanistan…twice. I have seen
an up-close and personal view of a hut on Bagram Air Base (Afghanistan) courtesy of Skype. I have anxiously followed news reports from the
Middle East. I have felt the nerves kick in when word came of a casualty,

and I have had relieved conversations with my mom when we found out that my brother was okay.

The Stars and Stripes fly boldly in front of my house. I have a yellow ribbon on my mailbox.

With my proud Southern roots, my family's service record, and my outward show of loyalty, I thought I knew what patriotism really was.

Until recently.

In August 2011, I sat in the memorial service for Navy SEAL Aaron Carson Vaughn, the very first military funeral I ever attended, and I thought, "So this is what sacrifice really looks like."

Somehow, in spite of my brother's involvement, I had been able to keep some form of emotional distance from the war. In many ways it felt so far removed from my everyday reality. Afghanistan is a long way from the football games, school work, doctor's appointments, grocery stores, and endless piles of laundry that consume my world as a wife and a mother to four boys.

That distance began to be bridged as I sat in Aaron's service and listened to his family and friends tell the story of a truly extraordinary man. The war had come home.

In a casket.

My heart bled in the beautifully awful moment when his mother was presented with a Gold Star. So much pain. So much pride.

Something began to shift inside of me that day.

It is still shifting.

Suddenly, I had to know everything I could about the American soldier. Not the surface stuff...the nitty-gritty. What makes people willing to lay their lives on the line? What kind of training do they go through? What is it really like to go to war? To stare death in the face? To lose your best friend on the battlefield?

If they had to endure these experiences, it seemed the very least I could do was learn everything that I could about them. My book list became about all things military. Want to know about the training of a

Special Ops warrior? Read pretty much anything by Dick Couch. I was mesmerized by every aspect of what these soldiers do to prepare themselves to fight the enemy.

And then I read *Lone Survivor* by Marcus Luttrell. The book gutted me. Completely gutted me. Through the words of Mr. Luttrell and the death of Aaron, the war was given a face and emotions. It no longer felt far away. It felt personal.

Because there is nothing more personal than someone's lifeblood being shed. For a fellow soldier. For the God-given right to live free. For the just cause of eradicating terrorism. For me.

I have come to realize that I did not have a clue about the true meaning of patriotism, but I am catching on.

Patriotism looks like Billy and Karen Vaughn—salt-of-the-earth, genuine people who raised an incredible young man and shared him with their country in his life and continue to share him with us in his death. Their faith is deep and calls us all to the realization that God is trustworthy even when life deals you the most difficult of blows.

It looks like Kimberly Vaughn, who is channeling her grief to urge us all to a deeper love of God and country. And to ensure that the memory of Aaron as a "warrior for Christ" is kept alive for his children.

I can't take away all of the rhetoric that is being thrown around. I can't take away the hurt that our men and women in the US Armed Forces, and their families, feel when they hear the verbal assaults against them.

But I will add my voice to the mix and yell at the top of my lungs, "Thank you! Thank you for your sacrifice on behalf of our great country."

To anyone who has ever laced up a pair of combat boots. To anyone who has ever left family and friends behind for a higher calling. To anyone who has tucked children in at night and then went to bed to cry alone because the pain of missing a spouse was so deep that it ripped at their very soul. To anyone who has cried out to God for the safety of a child on the battlefield. To anyone who has ever received "that call"... and heard the words that spun their world out of control. To anyone who has ever pounded a Trident into the unforgiving wood of a coffin. To anyone who has ever given one last salute to a fallen comrade.

Thank you.

Words are inadequate in the face of such noble actions, but sometimes they still need to be said.

A Special Note to Moms
by Karen Vaughn

W E'RE IN A WORLD OF hurt these days, aren't we? Struggles lurk at every turn. Big struggles. Complicated struggles. The world we grew up in *is* no more. Right is wrong, good is evil, up is down, left is right. And if we disagree with this new mindset, we're considered to be unenlightened, ignorant bigots.

Good grief! My head spins just thinking about it.

Our culture is hurtling out of control like a semi without brakes in the Rocky Mountains.

This big, bustling ball of twenty-first-century turmoil isn't the white picket fence fantasy life we imagined when we were still dressing up our Barbie dolls. But it's manageable.

Until we bring children into it. A child changes everything.

★

Two years ago a friend of mine, retired Green Beret Scott Mann, asked me a simple, yet life-altering, question: *"If you could do anything with your story, Karen, what would it be?"*

I had never pondered that thought. I had spent the previous four years in what seemed like a blur—spun up in a *story* that had a life of its own. A story that took this mother of three and grandmother of six across the nation, through the halls of Congress, into a National Press

Club conference, and onto multiple national television sets and dozens of radio programs. A story that gave me the platform to not only become a contributing columnist for two major conservative media outlets but also a national speaker and advisor for a veteran-driven advocacy organization. A story that ultimately placed me across the table from the war hero who asked me that thought-provoking question, one I now needed to answer: *What would I do if I could do anything with my story?*

And the first person I thought of was you.

You brave souls who brought a child into this crazy, spiraling out of control, upside-down world. You blessed women who understand the immeasurable joy *and* intense fear that come with parenting that precious bundle of joy—wondering if you've got what it takes to make your kid turn out right.

So, what launched this life-altering story?

In 2011 I lost my only son, US Navy SEAL Aaron Carson Vaughn, to the War on Terror. He gave his life fighting to protect and defend our nation—our way of life. In addition to his father and me plus his two sisters, he left behind a wife and two small children.

I've been told that moms won't want to read a story about a woman who lost her son. None of us want to contemplate what that reality would look like. It's too raw. Too painful.

But this isn't a book about loss; this is a book about life. A life so well lived that it left a legacy—a presence that took on a life of its own. When history is written, don't we all want the same to be said of our children?

The book you're about to read had already been written before I ever understood its God-given purpose. Not long after Aaron's death, I started jotting down everything I could remember about our life with Aaron. I wanted his children to know him. I wanted them to be able to laugh along with the stories that they should have heard *him* tell. I wanted them to have a record, if you will, of who he was and how large he lived. Something tangible they could pick up any time they needed to feel close to their dad and read or re-read a thousand times. I especially wanted them to see Aaron through my eyes so they could understand the magnitude of this man who—cradle to grave—elevated everyone he knew to a higher form of living.

When I looked back through the pages of what I wrote in those days following Aaron's death, I realized those very stories I had collected contained a thread, an intricate image of the making of a man who became a world changer. With that realization came the understanding that I wanted to share my story with you. I had already spoken to a few mom's groups and recognized that what I had experienced was valuable. I certainly do not claim the title of "perfect mom," but I have learned a lot and firmly believe that one of the best ways we, as mothers, learn from each other is by simply communicating with each other.

Your children's lives are packed with teachable moments. Aaron's was no different. While this book is based on the forging of a young man who ultimately became one of America's most elite warriors, I encourage you to look between the lines for *your* story…*your* family. Search out the truths that apply to *your* world. I urge you to immerse yourself in not only the triumphs but also the pains because life's greatest lessons are often filtered through the lens of deep, personal loss.

Raising great kids—kids with purpose—legacy-leaving kids—is completely possible. However, greatness never emerges from complacency. It's hard work. We moms are among those blessed enough, and trusted enough by God, to shape the future. Our children *are* the future. Don't ever forget that.

You are raising the future.

Be diligent.

I've been asked many times how we raised a man with such an indomitable spirit—how we brought up a boy so courageous that he willingly gave his life for a cause greater than himself.

I decided to think those questions through and transfer my genuine thoughts to the page. In the back of this book, you'll find a study guide that will help you evaluate this story in a different light. I pray you'll find it helpful.

Part One
The Forging

Aaron (front) and his cousin Garrett—Aaron was always ready for combat.

Chapter One

A Rocky Start

IT WAS 1980: THE YEAR John Lennon died and Reagan defeated Carter; the year of button-down shirts and blazers, Rubik's Cubes® and cordless phones; the year the Raiders, Lakers, and Phillies dominated the sports world; and the year I fell in love with Billy Carson Vaughn.

We grew up in small, adjoining towns in Northwest Tennessee. We didn't have malls, theaters, or even fast-food joints to hang out in, so we had to be a little more creative. Weekend nights were spent cruising along the main street of *my* town—Union City—windows down, radios blaring. Along its curves were the strategic pit stops we would drive through slowly in hopes of running up on something, or more to the point, *someone* interesting. IGA Grocery was one of those stops.

I was parked there on a Friday night that May when Billy and I noticed each other across the lot. Instead of walking over to me himself, he sent a friend to my car to see if I would like to talk. His audacity made me smile.

Within weeks we became inseparable. So much so that when the time came for me to head off to college in the fall, I switched schools, choosing a campus less than half an hour away from our hometown.

Then, during my very first semester, I noticed some changes in my body. It wasn't long until I began suspecting I might be pregnant.

I remember the pain in my parents' faces as if it were yesterday. They were sad...and rightfully so. All their aspirations and plans for what I could have become, what I might have accomplished, began fading as that tiny pink line emerged on my drugstore pregnancy test. Those hopes disappeared completely when my mother, the first ultrasonographer in our little corner of the world, confirmed the pregnancy with a sonogram. There it was—in black and white—a tiny, beating heart.

My parents were liberal enough in their thinking to not force Billy and me into a shotgun wedding, but conservative enough to have taught me that abortion would never be an option.

And it wasn't.

The only decision I had to make was would I be a single mom or would I marry my child's father? In all honesty, there was no question. We would marry. We would honor God, even though we had made a mess of things.

And just like that, my destiny was sealed. Instead of spending those college-age years living large and answering to no one but myself, I became a wife.

I became a mother.

And as every mother worth her weight finds out immediately, I was no longer the center of my universe. Tan lines gave way to stretch marks, my once flat stomach morphed into a hilarious bulging ball of baby, and somehow I felt more alive, more beautiful, and more at peace than ever before.

Then finally, on June 24, 1981, a nine-pound, eleven-ounce, blond-haired, blue-eyed baby boy made his entrance into this world. Aaron Carson Vaughn.

And just like that, a girl became a woman—seconds before a mother's child, now a child's mother. As I held that beautiful baby to my chest, touched the tip of my nose to his, counted all ten fingers and all ten toes, I experienced a sensation foreign to anything I had ever known. It was still. It was perfect.

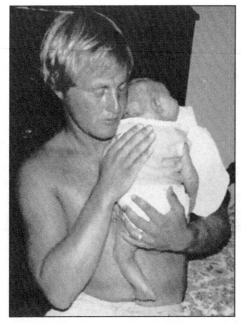

Billy in awe at his newborn son

It was *unconditional* love.

I saw the same in Billy's eyes. I watched in wonder as he tenderly brought Aaron's face to his shoulder—his strong hands cupping Aaron's neck, head, and bottom. The way he laid his cheek against Aaron's tiny face amazed me.

"Look at you two. Just look at you. Honey, you're a *daddy!*"

A profound bond had clearly been conceived, and nothing in Billy's life would ever be the same again.

As we stood over his crib that very first night after bringing him home from the hospital, we held each other tight in awe-struck wonder.

"Can you believe we're parents, Billy?"

"Not really. I still can't believe the hospital just let us take him home! We don't know anything!"

Billy was twenty-four, and I was only nineteen. We felt completely ill-equipped for the journey ahead, but we held on to each other and just kept walking.

I remember so many times in those first years when we would watch

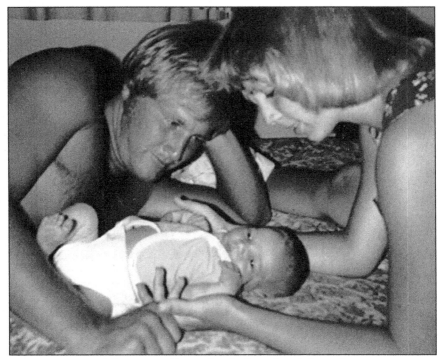

Billy, Aaron, and I on our first day home from the hospital

Aaron sleep and marvel at the thought that this amazing little man—hand-crafted by God—was ours. We felt so blessed to be entrusted with such an unspeakably precious gift.

At the time, our country was in a state of unrest. We had witnessed a recent assassination attempt on our sitting president and tensions between America and the Soviet Union were at their peak. Yet somehow, in our little corner of the world, we felt safe. We felt sheltered.

A family had been formed.

★

Since Aaron was not only our first child, but also the first grandchild on both sides of the family, you can imagine how full-steam-ahead the spoiling train ran. If that boy so much as grunted, someone had him in his or her arms immediately, and the circus would begin. Every adult in the room would then fully engage in the discovery and quick relief of his discontent. Somehow still, he was an exceptionally good baby, always

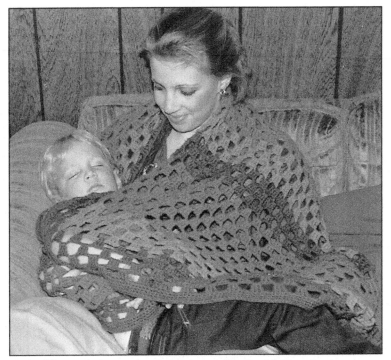

The cuddly years—There was no place Aaron would rather fall asleep than in my arms. And I loved every second of it.

happy, always smiling. I never took that for granted and was quick to thank God whenever it crossed my mind.

As a young mother, I especially treasured the fact that Aaron was a good sleeper and slept a lot. Years later, we would discover that he had suffered from allergies throughout his infant and toddler years, and the allergies kept him somewhat lethargic and less motivated than most boys his age. As a result, he spent a lot of time cuddling on our laps, learning that affection was healthy and that his parents represented love and safety.

I believe God used those very issues with Aaron's health as a way of forming him into the man he would be one day. During those years he became secure in kindness, gentleness, tenderness, and respect. As he grew older, he never once allowed others to make him think those attributes were un-cool. Instead, he *made* them cool. He had a way of rubbing off on a person like that.

Chapter Two

The Battle of Becoming

From the time Aaron could talk enough to genuinely express himself, it was clear that something was very different about him. He had a unique sense of discernment and a kind of nobility that seemed odd for such a young child. Billy and I worked hard to recognize, encourage, and reinforce those positive qualities in our son. Forging Aaron's heart into what would ultimately become the heart of a warrior was no simple task, but his father, Billy, is no simple man. He took the challenge of shaping his son's character seriously. Billy is cut from that rare cloth of true American patriots—a tough guy with a huge heart. He embodies courage and strength, but beneath that lays an artful blend of humility, a deep love for God, and a moral compass which never allows him to leave course. In other words, he had been born to be Aaron Vaughn's father. And, without a doubt, God clearly designated our small farm in rural Northwest Tennessee as the training ground on which Billy's purpose would be accomplished.

I grew up as somewhat of a city girl, so I cringed whenever Billy called Aaron outside to "help Daddy" with farm activities that I believed to be way beyond Aaron's level of maturity or physical capacity. My mother's heart was always at work attempting to protect my baby from the dangers lurking in every crevice of that farm. Billy's heart was driven to look for opportunities to teach Aaron how to be strong, fearless, gritty, and confident.

I remember walking out to the woods one day after the two of them had been working for many hours. In the distance, I could see Aaron, around eight years old, astride a four-wheel all-terrain vehicle, revving the engine. Only when I moved in for closer inspection did I notice the rope stretched between the rack on the revving four-wheeler and the thirty-foot tree Billy was cutting down with a chainsaw.

"Put it in gear and pull, Son."

My screeches of disbelief seemed to fall on deaf ears, but sheepish grins on both of their faces gave them away. They knew I had seen them.

While *I* didn't find that situation laughable, I tried hard to understand it from Billy's perspective. During the early years of our marriage, we had our share of confrontations over how to raise our children. Looking back, though, I'm glad my fears didn't stop Billy. Aaron was learning to overcome larger-than-life obstacles. With or without my nod of confidence in his father's judgment, he was being treated like a man rather than a boy.

The forging had begun.

It makes me smile to think about how fiercely I fought the forging. I actually battled it in every way I knew how, from dressing Aaron head-to-toe in solid white outfits to entering him in the Troy Tiny Tot Beauty Review—which, by the way, he won but never forgave me for. A dash of pride mixed with a little shame blushes my cheeks when I think about that less-than-honorable moment in parenting. But the pictures were worth all the grief I took—they offered me a ton of leverage through the teenage years.

★

Nearly all cattle farmers can attest to having a cow or bull in their herd that quickly earns a reputation as a troublemaker. On the Vaughn farm, that cow was named White Cow. She earned her complex and well-thought-out moniker from Aaron and his younger sister Tara, who were

His very own 4-wheeler—We had it hidden in a shed for quite some time and he "accidentally" found it before we could surprise him at Christmas. If that thing could talk, oh, the tales I'm sure it would tell!

Tara and Aaron crowned king and queen of the Troy Tiny Tot Beauty Review.

terrified to even make eye contact with her, much less stand in her presence.

In order to understand the dynamics at work, you need to know that we raised White Cow from the time she was a tiny calf. She had grown up on our farm. She was the boss. A living, breathing bovine dictator. For some reason, she decided early on that this farm belonged to her. Therefore, anyone who stepped foot on her farm, without her expressed approval, deserved to suffer her wrath. With huge horns and ridiculously long, floppy ears, this Brahman cow would paw the dirt, snort and shake her head, then charge the fence if we had the audacity to walk out of our back door. Her snorts and snarls allowed her to maintain perfect control over the Vaughn siblings' comings and goings on her forty-seven-acre dynasty.

The entertaining stories of White Cow's attitude and antics have circled our table for years. Our favorite one revolves around the life lesson Billy insisted on teaching Aaron sometime around his tenth birthday.

We were corralling the cattle that day, and Aaron's job was to stand by the open gap and then quickly shut the gate when the last cow entered the pens.

Billy coached Aaron: "Stand your ground, Son. If White Cow charges you, just punch her in the face!"

I watched with trepidation as the herd moved toward the pens, trying my hardest to stay out of this and to keep my mouth shut. Aaron, doing his dead-level best to trust his father, began swaying from side to side, nervously shaking out his tiny hands and then tightening his fists until his knuckles lost all color.

We all knew that White Cow saw Aaron as a challenge—one she believed she could win since he couldn't have weighed more than eighty pounds soaking wet. Finally, White Cow made her predictable move. Pawing the dirt, her head dropped, and she charged my baby.

To my utter astonishment, Aaron stood his ground, jerked his tiny little arm back in nerve-racking defiance, and punched that heifer square in the nose.

Stunned—and seemingly humiliated—White Cow staggered backward, dropped her head, and with her first-ever act of compliance, entered the pen behind the other cows, but not before she gave one final horn-shaking threat to let Aaron know she may be down, but she wasn't out.

I think Aaron was as stunned as his bovine nemesis, but he had done it! He had defeated White Cow! This enormous victory was a juncture in time which deserved slow-motion replays and possibly even fireworks as a fitting commemoration. Although the cameras weren't there to capture that glorious triumph, the moment was properly celebrated later when Aaron rode with his dad to the market one day, and White Cow became a pot roast. From then on, a huge grin of conquest plastered Aaron's face at the mention of her name.

That story is just one glimpse of many similar stories about life on our farm. Aaron was becoming—with or without my help—that strong, fearless, confident son his father had envisioned since he first lifted him to his chest and gazed into those huge, hope-filled eyes.

When Aaron was about eight years old, he started telling anyone who would listen, "One day I'm going to be a Navy SEAL." God had used Billy—and the time he and Aaron spent together taking care of the cattle and our farm—to plant that dream.

One afternoon, while Billy and Aaron were out on the farm patching fences, they had the truck radio on keeping them company. Someone on air mentioned the Army Rangers, and Aaron asked his dad about the Rangers and what they did.

Billy answered with a statement that ultimately shifted the course of our family's history: "Son, the Rangers are really tough, but there's a group of men out there who are a little tougher because they work on the land, in the air, *and* in the water. They're called Navy SEALs."

Something in his father's words stirred Aaron's eight-year-old mind, and just like that, his future was determined.

★

Over the years, I had to continuously remember to let Aaron be a boy and to allow him to pursue his huge, crazy dreams. I watched in fear, biting my lip, while his daddy turned him loose on three-wheelers and unsaddled colts and later with fireworks, BB guns, and then rifles. By the time Aaron was ten, he was driving a truck around the farm to help with all the daily chores.

Billy worked very hard to grow Aaron into a young man while I wanted so desperately to protect him, to do everything in my power to build a wall around him that could never be penetrated by danger. The thought that the fragile little lives of my beautiful children were in my hands completely overwhelmed me. At times the thought would literally keep me awake at night. This stress was intensified when it came to Aaron because he had such a perfect innocence about him, an innocence which demanded protection.

I still chuckle thinking back on the morning his little sister, Tara, two years his junior, told him the truth about the Tooth Fairy. In total incredulity, he bolted to my side and grabbed my leg, screaming.

"Uh-uh, you're lying, Tara. Shut up! Tell her to shut up, Mom!"

Tara, finding his reaction hilarious screamed back, "There's no Santa Claus either, Aaron!"

The dam broke.

While his heart was fierce and fearless, it was equally innocent and tender. That pure, unadulterated tenderness was a gift, one that surged through his veins until the day he left this earth.

✳

In the midst of those fear-ridden years, while toiling to fortify that bulwark around my babies, God brought Sara Williams into my life. She became a very dear friend who, as it turned out, taught me one of the most valuable lessons I ever needed to learn.

While patiently listening to me vent my fears during a heart-to-heart conversation one day, Sara finally interrupted me, looked me straight in the eye, and with great tenderness began explaining to me that my children were not my possessions. They belonged to God. They were on loan to me. Yes, they had been entrusted to me to care for, love, teach, and protect, but ultimately their lives were in God's hands, not mine.

With gentle, carefully chosen words, Sara taught me that God knew them before they ever were, He loved them more than I ever could, and He alone was responsible for the number of breaths they would draw on this side of eternity. I will never forget the simplicity of her confidence.

"Only God is with them everywhere they go…every minute of every day. You, my friend, are not."

Her words prompted me to contemplate how futile it was to think I had the power to keep them alive. What a ridiculous, arrogant concept to give myself so much credit for another's well-being. In the long run, that life lesson gave me the strength to allow the forging to continue.

And so it did…

Chapter Three:

Childhood Joys

NESTLED COMFORTABLY ON OUR SMALL farm in Northwest Tennessee, our children grew up surrounded by an extraordinarily loving family, a tight-knit community, and many close friends. Their lifestyle was truly something to be envied, and the memories of those years run deep.

Billy was always content with earning the family's living and allowing me the privilege of being a stay-at-home mom. At times I took jobs of my own to bolster our income, but those stints never lasted long. I would find myself overwhelmed with guilt, feeling like I was somehow failing in my *real* job, my *real* calling, which was—in my mind—raising my children. I wanted to take my kids to school each morning. I wanted them to know that *I* would be in carline picking them up each afternoon. I also wanted them to know that if they needed me at any time during the day, all they had to do was call. We sacrificed a lot to give our kids that kind of stability but felt content in doing so.

Being a stay-at-home mom also lent itself to a great deal of fun, especially when the kids were out of school.

On a typical summer day, I met up with two or three of my friends and their kids at one of the neighborhood pools. All of us moms would busy ourselves with sunbathing and catching up on our latest magazines

A family picnic when we were all so very young

and gossip while our kids splashed about enjoying a refreshing break in the hot, humid Tennessee summer. But before long, the kids would no longer be content with letting us moms just rest. (I'm sure you can relate!)

"Call it out, Mom!"

"Yeah, call it out, Mrs. Karen!"

I knew what they meant. The kids would line up on the scorching concrete with the only relief coming from the water cooling the ground as it dripped off their soaking wet bodies. One at a time, they would step onto the diving board and run towards the end. As their feet planted for the final push off from that floppy, rough surface, I would call out a challenge:

"Cannonball!"

"Swan dive!"

"Can opener!"

As soon as they came up for air, they would sling their wet faces straight toward us moms and wait for their score.

"Whoa, that was most definitely a 10!"

"I don't know, I'd call it an 8.5."

"Oh, come on!"

At some point, the heat would become too much for all of us moms. We would put our magazines down and let the kids take *their* turn making the calls and divvying out the points. And they never took it easy on us. Those days were full of love and laughter and are among some of my sweetest memories.

Usually, the fun spilled over to the local ballpark where, as the sun set, we would all come together again while the kids played ball with or against each other. In our world, everyone brought their own lawn chairs and coolers, but the unspoken rule was "this is community and what's mine is yours." Most of us were not people of means, but that actually fostered our sense of community because we all understood need and were quick to meet, on each other's behalf, any that arose among us. We cheered for each other's children and enjoyed their victories like they were our own. If someone took a head dive into home plate, ten moms—or dads—rushed the field. We were invested in each other, and our kids knew it.

We were family.

Aaron clearly embraced the simplicity of our lifestyle, and it was evident that he was secure in the deep love Billy and I had for him, with or without luxuries. He always described himself as *lucky*, a term that melted my heart. As my children grew into adults, they would often talk about those financially lean years as the best of their lives.

✶

Aaron and his sister, as well as their cousins and friends, knew the meaning of good, clean fun—the kind where, if you're not completely filthy at the end of the day, something didn't go right. They explored every ridge of our farm, every tree they could climb, every vine that would hold their weight—or not—and every inch of crystal clear creek bed. It all became a part of who they were. The dirt on that land embedded in their very core. It not only stained their clothes, but it also stained their souls.

So much so that Aaron took the farm with him whenever he could. Sharon Regen, Aaron's third-grade teacher at Hillcrest Elementary School, sent this tender letter to me on August 6, 2014, three years after Aaron's death:

I never knew what Aaron was going to bring to class. First, it was a frog in a dress shirt box. The poor thing was making soooo much noise I decided to let the LITTLE thing out. A bullfrog the size of a baseball leaped out and into my jumper pocket as I screamed and made a fool of myself...but to Aaron's delight.

Aaron and our pot-bellied pig

I had to check his backpack daily because I never knew what was going to be in it. One day he asked me if he could bring his pig to school to show everyone. I thought he just had a normal pig so I said no because we could see pigs from the playground. Aaron, with those big eyes, looked at me and said, "But my pig is special because he can do tricks and he lives in our house." I had no idea what a pot-bellied pig was so I was expecting this big old pig the next day. I could hear it squealing as it came down the hall begging for frosted flakes. All Aaron said was "I told you he was special." Aaron was the special one, and I will never forget him or those special times with him.

On another occasion, I was dropping Aaron off at school after a dental appointment, and while signing him in at the front office, Mrs. Regen walked by.

"Aaron, honey, why is your backpack dripping?" she asked.

When I heard her question, I looked down and noticed a trail of water leading all the way out the front door to our car. When I checked Aaron's backpack, I discovered an ice cream bucket full of tadpoles.

"I'm sorry, Momma! I had to leave the lid off so they could breathe."

"But why on earth did you bring them to school, honey?"

"Because I knew you'd throw them out if I left them in my room!"

I had a hard time getting mad about that excuse because he was probably correct and he was so dang adorable!

It was always something with Aaron, but Aaron's "somethings" were always comical.

One of our favorite stories revolves around the time Aaron accidentally shot his cousin. Billy had bought Aaron his very first Red Ryder BB Gun, a pump-action gun, and Billy had given careful instruction to never pump the gun more than twice. Well, one day, while playing at the barn, Aaron decided to pump the gun six times instead. Then he promptly tripped, fired the gun, and shot his cousin Courtney in the back as she was climbing a gate.

Outside our back door

In quick reaction to her writhing pain, Aaron bolted for the house. By the time Courtney and her huge red welt arrived, Aaron's case for innocence was in full deliberation.

"I didn't mean to, Mom!"

"Didn't mean to what, Son?"

"Shoot Courtney! It was an accident, I swear. I don't even know how the gun went off!"

On many occasions, Billy and I had a terrible time keeping straight faces while hearing Aaron's descriptions of "accidents" and other negative incidents. With total sincerity, he would say things like *"Tara's face just ran into my hand. I don't know how it happened"* or *"she was running by, and my foot just jerked and tripped her."* Body parts or inanimate objects were almost always liable. He was creative, to say the least.

But don't get me wrong, Billy and I didn't simply laugh these things off. We chuckled *privately* at Aaron's weak attempts to circumvent what he knew was coming. We did *not* laugh at what he had done. We took our parenting seriously. We were keenly aware that discipline was necessary and that Aaron needed to understand that actions create consequences. We made a concerted effort to be creative and effective with our forms of discipline, and we were never shy about using them. Of course, in the shooting incident, the gun was taken away for quite some time. As hard as it was to seize the gun when he had just received it, we felt that this was the right thing to do. Until he could treat the gun with the level of respect it deserved, it would remain in our closet.

★

On more than one occasion Aaron and Tara's childhood antics nearly cost me my sanity. One day, as I was just about to jump in our downstairs shower, I realized they were both outside on the 4-wheeler. Deciding I wanted them to park the 4-wheeler until I was done showering, I grabbed a towel, threw it around me, and ran outside…barefoot.

As soon as I opened the back door, I could hear a faint, weak voice in the distance yelling "Help…Mom….Help."

Terrified, I took off running. I crested the second ridge from our house before I saw them both lying in the field, the 4-wheeler flipped on its top. Rushing to them, screaming for a response, I saw Aaron motionless and Tara crying.

My heart nearly stopped.

Long story short, they were both fine. Aaron was pretending to be knocked out cold for fear of what I would do when I found out he had been letting his little sister drive. I guess he thought his chances to evade punishment would be greater if I thought he was unconscious.

Only after my wheezing sigh of relief did I realize that I was standing in the middle of my farm with no shoes…and no clothes.

We made a million memories on that farm, and it seemed like there was never a dull day or night.

★

In celebration of Aaron's tenth birthday, he and his friends decided they wanted to camp out in our woods. (Aaron had no idea just how dark those woods would become after the sun set and daddy went into the house.) We spent the whole day prepping the area, shopping for the perfect junk food, pitching the tent, and getting everything just right.

Twenty minutes after being out there, Aaron came inside and asked, "Hey, Mom, would it be alright if we moved out of the woods and pitched the tent right behind the barn?"

"Sure, Son, what's wrong?" I was secretly smiling.

"Oh, nothin'. It's just a long walk to the house from back there."

About an hour later, Billy woke me up after he did a quick check on the boys. Laughing under his breath, he said, "You've got to come see this."

The boys had moved their tent all the way up to the gate that separated our yard from the farm. We had a good laugh and went back to bed.

I woke up in the middle of the night and decided to just take a quick glance to make sure everything was still okay. This time they were *in the backyard, directly outside the back door!* I could barely contain my laughter.

Billy and I teased Aaron mercilessly the next day, but he defended his actions with wide eyes and an anxious tone. "Dad, seriously! There was something trying to get in our tent last night, and every time we moved, it followed us! It was snortin' and pushin' on the edges right at the ground. Like it was trying to lift the tent up."

Billy cracked up. "Son, that was probably Simon (our pot-bellied pig). He roots at everything! Especially when he smells food."

Never a dull moment.

★

We had bonfires in the fall, went sledding down the large rolling hills in the winter, and 4-wheeled through the hay-covered fields, poplar-canopied woods, and crystal clear creek beds year round. All that our kids needed could be found on that tiny parcel of land God gave us as their stomping ground—their base. They were happy children.

And me? I tried as best I could to allow my kids the opportunity to be just that—kids. I knew adventure and risk were *both* necessary for the development of courage, strength, and independence. I also knew failure had its place. How can anyone truly appreciate victory without having had a good dose of defeat? I was learning to let go, and they were learning to thrive.

Chapter Four

Realities of Life

As the endless rotation of time continues, most of us experience hitches that throw us off course, at least momentarily. The Vaughn family snags came wrapped in both great blessing and great pain.

By the time Aaron hit his pre-teens, he and his little sister witnessed first-hand the devastating indifference and depravity of mankind. Their first encounter with pain revolved around an adoption attempt on our family's part, which instead of ending in a happy adoption ended in an abrupt, unexpected, heartbreaking abortion.

This was a crucial point in Aaron and Tara's spiritual development. They were deeply and personally aggrieved by the choice this young mother made to terminate the life of their would-be little brother or sister. They had already made plans and picked out names. The mother's decision was a cruel interruption of their hopes and expectations for what could have been—what should have been. Their tender little eyes filled with anguish as I explained what had happened.

"I'm so sorry. I tried to stop her. I begged her not to go through with the abortion, but I couldn't change her mind."

"Why would she do that?" Tara asked.

"I don't know, sweetie. I can't explain it."

Aaron's words cut straight to the heart of it—"She just killed him?"

It was hard to defend, because there was no defense. I wrapped my arms around them both, and we cried.

Although Aaron and Tara had formed a personal relationship with Christ by then, I believe they began viewing humanity in a somewhat different light after that day. The lesson we tried to teach them was simple: people are not perfect, but God is. He is the only One who will never fail or forsake us. And yes, sometimes He allows terrible things, but He alone knows why and He can be trusted.

Then came the blessing. After years of prayer, unable to have any more children on our own, God laid Ana Marie Vaughn in our arms through a private adoption. We brought her home when she was only seven months old.

Aaron, Tara, and Ana in the Woodland Mills, Tennessee, Christmas Parade

Those first few weeks after Ana's arrival were magical. Aaron was almost twelve, and Tara was ten. Because of their ages, they acted more like parents than siblings. They couldn't get enough of this new wonder now crawling the floors of our home, giggling and cooing her way into our hearts. The two of them often fought over who got to rock her to sleep at night. Watching them embrace our perfect little addition with zero resentment or hesitation was a precious sight. Ana completed our family, and life was wonderful.

But this euphoria would prove to be short-lived. Unbeknownst to us, unspeakable darkness lay just beyond view. Within months of our family's highest high, we experienced the darkest year we had known to date.

There are moments in time when a transformation takes place, and nothing is ever the same again. In the scientific world, these pivotal junctures are known as paradigm shifts. And, boy, were we about to experience one.

Our shift came in the form of a church split.

Unwittingly, we became targets by association to the most brutal onslaught of condemnation I had ever witnessed in or out of the church. Somehow the decision was made that certain families in our small-town, close-knit body posed a threat to the changes a new pastor sought to implement. And, quite literally, all hell broke loose. Only Satan himself could have orchestrated the ensuing scenario.

I'm not sure that anyone involved truly understood what was happening or why. Insults begat deeper, more personal insults, and as integrities were questioned, accusations flew. Lifelong relationships, as well as the people behind them, were demolished. These gut-wrenching displays of human weakness must incomprehensibly grieve the heart of God, so I will not expound further. Those who have endured a church split may grasp the magnitude of what we lived. (I struggled greatly over whether to discuss this portion of our life at all, but its value in building Aaron's character could not be denied.)

Through this disruption, we lost nearly every friend with whom we had previously shared the most intimate parts of our lives. We had no more days at the pool. The once thriving-with-life ballpark became a place of finger-pointing, torment, and excruciating isolation for us as well as all the children caught in the crossfire. Our kids and others were mocked in their school classrooms by students and—believe it or not—even one of their teachers. And tragically, Aaron and Tara were repudiated by their once loving church youth ministries, of which they had been a fundamental part. (Ana was still an infant, so, thankfully, she was unaffected.)

It was as if the lights had gone out. Our storybook life had ended.

As Billy and I pondered these things in our hearts, we often referred to this monumental overturn as something akin to losing your entire family in a moment's flash.

In the wake of this unprecedented cruelty at the hands of people our family had once trusted, Aaron and Tara had a decision to make...a profound one, an essential one. They needed to determine, right then and there, whether their trust rested in the church and its people or in God and God alone. Their entire identities and everything they believed hung in the balance. Rather than becoming bitter, as could have been expected, the two of them became grounded, determined, and serious about the concept of righteousness. I'm not saying they didn't struggle—they did. They were forced to build new friendships, find new activities to engage in, and re-define the life they had previously lived. Recovering from this whole situation was an unimaginably painful process which took years of healing to completely overcome, but it had its place in their development and ultimately did the work God intended it to do.

Remember the affliction I lived with—my desperate desire to protect my children? There was no need to fret. Looking back, I can see that God, in His sovereignty, wanted Tara and especially Aaron to experience every drop of our church split. He wanted Aaron to understand, fully recognize, and *despise* injustice. God wanted to teach Aaron about the glorious reward of standing for right even when, or *especially* when, all others run in fear. But mostly, I believe He wanted to teach Aaron the principle of the lukewarm: that those who are neither hot nor cold are of all men most desolate. (Revelation 3:15-17)

Billy wasn't the only one forging our son's heart. Our great God was most definitely at work. He saturated my dry, fragile spirit with this promise: "What Satan meant for evil, I meant for good."

Our warrior's heart was being consecrated.

Chapter Five

The World around Him

A<small>ARON WAS A BOY WHO</small> loved fun and games, yet he also had a serious, tender side to his personality. He possessed an extraordinary capacity for love and respect and bore an innate burden for the downtrodden.

One of the most amazing acts of kindness I have ever witnessed came through Aaron's hands.

We were on our way home from Nashville's Youth Evangelism Conference with a busload of teenagers when we stopped at a fast-food restaurant for a very late meal. The kitchen staff planned to close the restaurant as soon as our last teenager was served. As usual, Aaron waited in the back of the line. If someone were going to miss out on being served, it would be Aaron. He would make sure of it.

Aaron and I talked as we waited…and waited…and waited for our turn. At one point I heard a few awkward chuckles coming from the dining area where some of the teens were seated. I glanced around and noticed an elderly, poorly dressed, and very disheveled-looking man walking around inside the restaurant. He appeared to be slightly disoriented, too. I was a little bothered by our teens' somewhat rude reactions, but with my stomach growling and my full focus on satisfying that hunger, I didn't give the situation much attention.

After a while, Aaron and I ordered our food, and as expected, the kitchen closed the minute we received it. With my meal in hand, I headed straight to an open table to devour my sandwich. As I sat down, I noticed Aaron hadn't followed, so I started searching the restaurant to see where he had gone.

"Are you looking for Aaron, Mrs. Karen?" One of the teens asked and then pointed to the front of the restaurant, just beyond the glass. "He's out there."

Aaron was outside with that same homeless man who was now sitting on the front sidewalk. I hadn't even paid attention to where the man had gone. I had ignored him, but it was not in Aaron's DNA to do the same. My heart was moved with a strong blend of guilt and pride as I watched Aaron hand the man his food. All of it.

But Aaron wasn't finished.

He not only fed the man physically, but he also spent the next fifteen minutes sharing the love of Christ with the battered, old, broken man that the rest of us had ignored and rejected. I watched from behind as Aaron's arms flowed through gestures I recognized well, the old gentleman staring into Aaron's eyes and nodding with understanding. Aaron pointed to the sky then touched his heart. When his strong hands formed the shape of a bridge, I knew exactly where he was in the story.

I was never more proud of anyone in my entire life.

Unbeknownst to Aaron, the whole restaurant watched in silence. When he finally came back inside, I offered to share my food. He refused. He wanted to experience the sacrifice. He wanted to give without receiving anything in return.

This was Aaron Vaughn at his finest. He was a boy *any* mother would be proud to call son.

I couldn't tell you how many times Billy and I were applauded for how respectful, compassionate, and well-mannered Aaron was. He was a young man who honored those in authority over him and had no problem submitting and even humbling himself to those authority figures. With that humility came a heart filled with genuine kindness. He was happy to place others before himself, and in fact, he found great reward in doing so.

Looking back now, I believe a lot of Aaron's character traits and his personality that made him seem almost larger than life at times took root in what Billy and I chose to *emphasize* with our kids. We taught Aaron, as well as Tara and Ana, to say "ma'am" and "sir." We didn't teach this because we wanted people to feel old but because we wanted them to feel respected. And as we demanded our children use those terms when addressing adults, the sense that adults were to *be* respected grew organically. With that constant training in Aaron's early years, respect and compassion for his father and I as well as other adults had become second nature by the time he moved into his teens.

★

As I said earlier, Aaron's healing from our church split took some time. He suffered through some serious struggles over that life-altering event. But God was not about to let that boy, or the rest of us, lose hope. God sent us a miracle.

His name was Reverend Jimmy Brown.

Sometimes the only one who can really minister to a wounded soul is someone whose soul itself has been wounded. When Jimmy first visited our family to invite us to his church, I found him to be a kind, yet stoic man. Though I couldn't put my finger on it, I knew something was very different about him. I was captivated by the unyielding capacity he possessed to befriend, love, and care for the broken. For us.

In the subsequent days, weeks, and months, the body of believers at Pleasant Hill Baptist Church drew us under their wings. They bandaged our wounds and set us on our feet again. In a million years, I could never repay the people of that tiny country church for what they gave my family—a place of hope, a place of refuge, and a place of healing.

Aaron became close friends with the Brown's youngest son Josh and subsequently ended up becoming close to Brother Jimmy and his wife, Judy. Aaron spent a lot of time at their home being cared for and loved.

They treated him like family. These precious people and their capacity for love restored Aaron's and Tara's trust in church leadership.

After getting to know the Browns, we learned where all their grace and tenderness came from—a place of personal grief which we had no way of comprehending at the time. The year before we met them, their teenage son Doug had tragically lost his life. I cannot fathom how they mustered the strength to care about and love on us while they, themselves, were in so much pain. But I am eternally grateful for their love and compassion.

★

Not long after our arrival at Pleasant Hill, we took a mission trip to West Virginia. On our team were many teenagers, as well as a few senior adults. As the week moved along, one of those seniors became quite agitated with the teenagers' antics and sense of humor, and this man freely expressed his agitation. One day while Mr. Prince was napping in a wingback chair, Aaron decided to have a little fun. He inked in Gorbachev's birthmark on the old man's bald head.

Mr. Prince then spent the rest of the day and night sporting the faux mark, murmuring and grunting, "What's wrong with you people? What's so funny?"

Hours passed before anyone gave it away. Once the cat was out of the bag, Mr. Prince got a good laugh out of it as did the rest of us.

That was our Aaron—always looking for a way to enjoy the moment and make others laugh. He definitely knew how to squeeze memorable fun out of any situation, and he was a total clown. Finding a picture of him during those years without a smile plastered across his face is nearly impossible. Laughter—and good-hearted mischief— defined his disposition.

★

Remember my description of Aaron's utter innocence, which followed him throughout his life? Here's a perfect illustration: Billy's sister, Kelly, and her family bought a portion of our farm not many years after we settled there. Their home was nestled at the edge of the woods near the southeastern corner of our farm. As Aaron grew, he saw their property as a training ground for developing his stealth Navy SEAL skills. He would slither out of the woods, belly-crawl to their family room or kitchen window and see how long it would take for someone to discover his presence.

I can still picture the perplexed look on his face the day I explained to him, "Son, you *could* crawl up there one day and see something you *may not want to see.*" As understanding finally flooded his eyes, I could tell that the thought had never crossed his mind. From then on, he made sure the whole family was home before he played any recon games at their windows. And, boy, did his recon games give us some good laughs over the years.

One late afternoon when Aaron was about fourteen, he came bursting through our back door and into the kitchen just as I was putting dinner in the oven. He could barely speak as he doubled over, one hand on his belly and one on his knee, laughing hysterically. I cracked up just watching him. After a few seconds, he gained his composure enough to tell me what had happened. Through waves of laughter, he explained that he had crept up to Kelly's dining room window during their mealtime.

"Mom, the window was cracked open just a little, and Trey...(laughter)...Trey was sitting right there with his back against it. So I got down right beneath the window...(laughter)...and burped real loud." Tears rolled out of the corners of his eyes, and he continued trying to catch his breath through his wheezing laughter. "Aunt Kelly thought it was Trey and got all over him. So I did it again. I just kept doing it over and over again, and Trey kept flipping around trying to see who it was, and Aunt Kelly just got madder and madder because Trey wouldn't admit he was doing it. Trey kept saying, 'It's not me, momma! I swear, it's not me!' And that just made her even more upset. I finally couldn't take it anymore and started laughing out loud. You should have seen it! Oh my gosh!"

On another occasion, he returned to our home laughing just as wildly as he told me how he had just slithered to the edge of their property to do surveillance on Uncle Larry, Kelly's husband, while he worked in the yard. With face painted and body covered with camouflage and leaves, Aaron laid in wait to once again see how long he could remain unnoticed. About fifteen minutes in, Larry walked to the edge of the woods. Thinking he had been discovered, Aaron was just about to stand when Larry began unzipping his pants to relieve himself. Aaron's laughter jolted him to a halt. "Whoa, whoa, whoa, Uncle Larry!"

★

Even with his crazy antics and pranks, Aaron still enjoyed nothing more than sitting at his father's feet for a good history lesson. His eyes would come to life as he and his dad discussed issues of the day and compared current policies to the intentions of our founders. Aaron's patriotism was remarkable, but it was taught—make no mistake about it. Our children were constantly made aware and reminded of the great prices paid by those who came before us, those who insured our freedom. They knew to place their hand over their hearts and stand at attention when the national anthem was sung or the Pledge of Allegiance spoken.

By his early teens, Aaron had clearly developed a keen awareness of world events and a strong desire to understand which world leaders were moving the chess pieces. While most kids his age couldn't tell you who the current President was, Aaron could name a good portion of his cabinet. Remember the story of Mr. Prince and the faux birthmark? What fifteen-year-old kid do you know who could draw Gorbachev's birthmark from memory or even tell you who Gorbachev was?

Back in fourth grade, when Aaron was interviewed by the local newspaper about tensions in the Middle East, he responded, "We shouldn't let them (Saddam Hussein) take over a lot of places....We should go over there for the sake of young people he's killing with gas." His warrior spirit was seeping through even then, and he was only nine. Little did any of us know at the time, Aaron would be part of the United States Armed Forces when Saddam Hussein was finally captured.

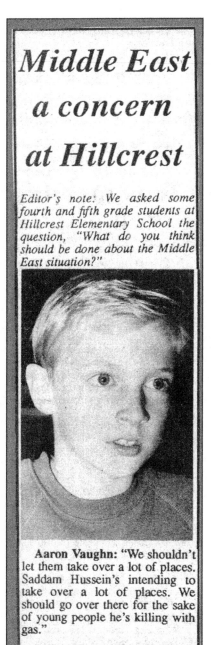

Middle East a concern at Hillcrest

Editor's note: We asked some fourth and fifth grade students at Hillcrest Elementary School the question, "What do you think should be done about the Middle East situation?"

Aaron Vaughn: "We shouldn't let them take over a lot of places. Saddam Hussein's intending to take over a lot of places. We should go over there for the sake of young people he's killing with gas."

The clipping from our local newspaper

What Aaron ultimately became was astonishing on many levels. From the first mention of his quest to become a Navy SEAL, no one ever believed a boy from Troy, Tennessee, could fulfill that dream. It was too big…too enthusiastic. I mean, a Navy SEAL? The chances of becoming an NFL football player were *much* better. However, Aaron never needed the confirmation of man. This matter had been settled in his heart from the beginning. Aaron knew what he was becoming. The rest of us couldn't see it, but Aaron could see it. And God could see it.

Our warrior was nearly forged.

Chapter Six

The Heart of a Teenager

THROUGHOUT AARON'S HIGH SCHOOL YEARS, a lot of outside factors shaped our son. It was a beautiful thing to watch. He was growing in his relationship with Christ, and therefore, keeping things healthy in his free time…for the most part. I'm not going to pretend he was impervious to trouble, but he chose friends wisely and stayed home a lot on weekend nights rather than running with the crowd. Aaron never got himself wrapped up in drama. He had a long-term vision and anything superfluous—or potentially posing a threat to his end game—would have to take a backseat.

While Aaron's heart was good-natured, full of fun, and brimming with integrity and kindness, he also had his faults. For instance, Aaron sometimes got carried away in his attempts to have a good laugh. On one occasion, he and his buddy Caleb decided it would be funny to shoot a bottle rocket into their football coach's office. Aaron's job was to get down on his belly, peer through the small space between the floor and the door and line up the projectile for ultimate impact. Caleb waited on his knees for his cue to light the fuse. But just as the fire ignited, one of the school principals rounded the corner. Even if the boys had wanted to, there was no turning back. Both met "The Board of Education" in

Coach Shank's office, but they swore the paddling was worth the great laugh they got.

Without a doubt, Aaron's high school teachers and administrators still relive the day when the windows of their classrooms rattled because of his science project. Aaron had built a volcano, filled with explosives he had collected from way too many disassembled fireworks. You can imagine what happened when the volcano erupted. He wasn't expelled, but by today's policies, he probably would have been arrested for the scare.

★

Perhaps Aaron's high school coaches recognized and knew some of his other faults the best.

During his freshman year, Aaron was cut from the basketball team for being too aggressive. Anyone who had ever played basketball with Aaron would absolutely understand that decision. Aaron wasn't cruel; he was simply too tenacious for the sport. The boy could not understand the foundational principle of the foul. It made no sense to him. If a ball was in play, wasn't it an obligation to do *everything* in your power to possess it? That is how his brain functioned—win or die trying. Aaron didn't believe in the middle ground. Consequently, he was much better suited for the football field.

Football became his life. In our hometown, that was a very good thing. If you've ever watched *Friday Night Lights*, you've seen a full-screen narrative of what it's like to grow up in Big Orange Country. On game day, checkered flags flap in the wind, moms sport their oversized "Proud Parent of #___" buttons, and any dad who is able squeezes himself into the sacrosanct letter jacket of his glory days. At game time, the stadium swells to standing room only as the National Anthem, sung by an upcoming local talent, sweeps across the field and into the bleachers, a brilliant crescendo of good ol' American pride. Politically correct or not, the whistle is never blown before the entire stadium bows for prayer.

Aaron loved this game.

And I loved watching him play it.

Aaron, wearing #1, was fierce on the football field.

GONNA GET 'YA — Obion Central junior defensive end Aaron Vaughn chases Gibson County quarterback Jason Hill out of the pocket in the final minutes of Friday night's game at Dyer. Vaughn had four tackles, two of those behind the line, as Central rallied from a 10-point deficit and then held on to claim a 27-20 win. Now 4-5, the Rebels will close the 1997 season with a Region 7-3A game at Brighton Thursday night.

He had intensity unlike any other on the field. His leg would literally quiver with anticipation before each snap of the ball. Being 6'4" but weighing only 160 pounds, Aaron's favorite compliment that he ever received came when he was named "Defensive Player of the Week" during his sophomore year. His coach described him to our local newspaper as "someone who played much bigger than his size."

The football field was my first insight into how very tough my boy was. Nothing stopped him. But even on the football field, he was sometimes given a hard time for his overachieving aggression.

On one occasion, we learned he had been tackling a teammate during a scrimmage with such force that the young man left the field and refused to return until the coaches "did something about Aaron."

Aaron was a sophomore, the teammate a senior. The coaches found it humorous and refused to discourage Aaron, but they *did* patiently explain that it probably wasn't a good idea to injure the starting quarterback. Aaron agreed but still struggled with the concept. In his mind, if you couldn't run with the big dogs, you should stay on the porch.

★

I would be remiss if I failed to mention two of the more difficult areas of Aaron's teenage years. Aaron *continuously* tested my patience in academics and organization. We had *many* battles over the condition of his bedroom, which I came to understand as simply par for the course when raising a teenage boy. However, his academic performance presented a much more complex challenge and couldn't be chalked up to simply being a teenager.

Early on, Aaron was tested and recommended for advanced placement due to his high I.Q. Knowing how smart he really was, it was distressing to watch him pull in less than stellar scores semester after semester. After countless discussions, endless negotiations, and knock-down drag-outs while trying to help him with his homework, I realized I was fighting a battle in which victory was subjective. The synaptic transmission had finally been processed—I was not raising a student; I was raising a warrior. Average grades would have to suffice. Over time, I slowly realized that Aaron's issue was not commitment; he just lacked commitment to anything he perceived as having no value for his end game of becoming a Navy SEAL. I needed a lot of faith to wrap my mind around his ultimate goal—his calling—but once I did, life was simplified.

As parents, we need to know how to choose our battles—you know, figure out what really matters, not to *us* but to *them*. A lot of us have plans for our kids. They're good plans, and there's nothing wrong with those plans. However, I've seen parents refuse to acknowledge the desires and gifts hidden in their children's hushed little mouths. If our children don't comply, we scold. And while scolding may be appropriate in many situations, we have to be careful to understand that it's not appropriate in all situations. My kids will probably tell you that the best gift I ever gave them was the gift of listening as they poured out their hearts. By listening, I was able to truly *know* them.

I'm not sure how many parents are afforded the luxury of honest, loving, open relationships with their children, but for those of you who've known that type of relationship, you know its value. A major part of my story—my heart and my loss—is difficult to share simply because it is so personal, but I feel like Aaron's story wouldn't be properly recorded if I left it unspoken.

Aaron always talked to me.

It sounds simple, but almost nothing I'll share about him more profoundly defines the love, the tenderness, and the sincerity of this child I was privileged enough to watch become a man. He *talked* to me from the time he was a very young child up until the time he left this earth.

Usually our talks would begin after everyone else went to bed. This is when Aaron did his deepest thinking—in the silence of the night. The conversations would start around 10 p.m. with "Hey, can I ask you something?" and end around 3 a.m. with "I love you so much, Son" and "I love you too, Mom."

For some reason, my opinion had weighted value for Aaron. In all humility, I never felt I deserved the right to guide this young man, one who clearly had a value system superior to most. But still, he trusted me, and the full measure of that gift was never lost on my heart. I trusted him, too. While firmly remaining his parent, I was always his friend.

Our long, late-night talks are treasures I'll hold in my heart for the rest of my time here on earth. During one of those talks, I led him through the sinner's prayer and watched in awe as my young son gave his heart and life to Jesus.

In those solemn hours of bonding, I labored with deep empathy over every disappointment and heartache that made its way into my boy's world. We talked of failures—mine and his. We spoke of overcoming. Together, we navigated the chaos and confusion of love gained and love lost. He shared his deepest fears and concerns, as well as his greatest moments of amusement, victory, and laughter. I'm sure he didn't tell me everything, but I was often surprised by the level of trust he offered me. I believe he always understood my love to be completely unconditional from the time he was born until the day he breathed his last.

I have wondered many times since Aaron's death why God chose to take *my* son, when his father and I shared such a healthy, loving relationship with him. I mean, couldn't He have taken someone who was monstrous to his parents, whose life brought grief rather than blessing? Any time that thought crosses my mind, I'm quickly admonished by the principle of II Corinthians 10:5b, which I utilized many times over the years to restore my children's discouraged hearts—"*We take captive every thought to make it obedient to Christ.*" As I remember those faithful words of healing, I heed their advice. Upon reconfiguration, that sometimes-crippling questioning looks more like this: Thank you, God, for a life of no regrets.

How inconsolable would I be today if our memories with Aaron were marked by unforgiven strife or unresolved disappointment?

Chapter Seven

New Places, New Faces

W HEN AARON WAS SIXTEEN, BILLY and I made the agonizing, yet hope-filled, decision to leave our lifelong home in Tennessee. The time had come for our family to follow a different path. For almost eleven months before our move, we prayed about our decision. It took more courage than we felt we could muster, but we knew in our hearts that God was leading us to move to Martin County, Florida. At the time, Aaron was in the middle of his junior year, Tara was a freshman, and Ana had just turned five.

Our journey south began on a cold winter afternoon in February 1998. After strapping little Ana into her booster seat and slamming the door on our moving van, we went to pick up Aaron and Tara from their last day of classes at Obion County Central High School.

The scene at the school that day was something I will never forget. As we drove into that familiar parking lot—the lot where even Billy had parked *his* truck during high school—there in the grassy lawn between the gymnasium and the first row of cars stood dozens of our children's closest friends. These were lifelong friends—ones they had started kindergarten with. These friends circled our precious kids, heads down, tears flowing, eyes revealing a state of disbelief that this was actually happening.

People don't move away from small towns in Tennessee. You're born there, and you die there. That's just the way it is.

With great sadness, Aaron and Tara finally crawled into the car, buckled up, and off we went. For several hours, complete silence enveloped us as we all contemplated how much of our lives was disappearing through our rear view mirror: grandparents, aunts, uncles, cousins, friends, and oh-so-many memories.

Our move was an incredibly pivotal time frame in our teenagers' lives. Again, they were left with choices. Would they embrace this journey with hope and anticipation, or would they scorn the uprooting with anger and bitterness? It does my heart good to tell you that they chose wisely. While Aaron and Tara found their new world to be quite a different experience from small town USA, they made it work.

Once we settled into our new life in Florida, we had no doubt that we were in the exact place God had chosen for us. A new chapter began, and we were certain it would be filled with purpose. One of our top priorities after moving was seeking out a new church. As believers in Christ, we have always understood the biblical principles God laid out regarding being part of a church family and how much value that family adds to your everyday existence. We wanted to find a church where Aaron and Tara would have a solid youth group—a support system plus a network of instant friends.

I remember the first night we met Rex and Marti Briant, youth pastors at First Baptist Church, Stuart. Even though we had visited the church on a few occasions, I knew our kids would never feel connected or make friends until they dove in headfirst. Wednesday night youth group was the only place that was going to happen.

So, one Wednesday evening, I decided to walk my kids into their first youth group meeting to make introductions and to size up their level of comfort before abandoning them to complete strangers. When we reached the front of the room, the entire assemblage, with Rex and Marti in the lead, circled Aaron and Tara, mesmerized by their thick southern drawls and beautiful faces. We still laugh as we recall a few of the students asking Aaron to repeat his name over and over.

"Arn."

"Are you saying Arn?"

"No—Arn."

"Sorry…Arn?"

"ARN."

I could hear the frustration in Aaron's voice, and I finally had to step in. "It's Aaron."

The girls grinned, the guys shook his hand, and the bonding began.

This youth group and its leaders quickly became Aaron and Tara's entire world. Only once in my lifetime have I witnessed such a powerful union of students and leaders who sincerely loved each other as much as they loved Christ. This was it. These new friends began filling every free hour of our two oldest children's lives. Deep, life-altering relationships were being conceived.

Rex and Marti weren't your average youth leaders. Although their home overflowed with a family of their own, their students were as much a part of their existence as their natural-born babies. On a typical Saturday, the entire youth group spent the morning at the beach for surf and sun and then headed to a park to play some flag football. Nightfall usually found them all at the Briant home, watching movies and eating pizza.

Rex was the epitome of a manly man. He had played football throughout high school and college and had brilliantly maintained his strong physique. He was handsome and quick with a smile, but his best attribute was his fierce love for Christ. He bonded with Aaron instantly, and more often than not, Rex was the one assigned to cover Aaron during those Saturday afternoon football games. During Aaron's memorial service in Florida, Rex shared the story of the first time he ever came up against Aaron in football:

"When it was time for my side to be on defense, we're all divvying up who we're going to cover. Nobody went over to Aaron's side. So *I* had to.

Of course, I was about thirty-seven at that point going against a sixteen-year-old spry young man.

"I remember the first play. I don't know *what* happened, but I never saw him go by me. I looked over my shoulder, and he had a ball in his hand, heading to the end zone. Well, I decided in my heart that *'there is no way this young man's gonna ever do that again on me.'* So, we spent the next hour and a half fighting for five yards.

"And the only way that whole skirmish ended was with me finally getting hurt and having to leave the field. And Aaron did it with total respect, by the way: 'Oh, Rex. I'm sorry!…Ohhhh, that must of hurt!…Ohhh.'

"I'd never prayed for an injury before in my life, but that day God gave me a blown hamstring, and I was grateful for it. It put me on the sideline. We finished the game, went home, and ate steaks."

This couple exemplified the way life should work and what marriage should look like. Aaron often told me "I want a family like theirs one day." I deeply loved the Briants for their willingness to embrace, nurture, and navigate my kids through what could have been a very difficult transition.

★

Aaron spent his first summer in Florida learning to have city fun. Still honing his stealth warrior skills, he would come home with hilarious stories of he and his friends—armed with air horns—slithering into the shrubs at several of the local golf courses. You can visualize the rest.

With the young men from his youth group, Aaron learned, among many other things, to explore and enjoy the endless mysteries of the great Atlantic Ocean. Being a farm boy all his life, the open water was new to him. His buddies still tell stories about their fear of Aaron drowning while learning to surf. The problem with Aaron was he would never give up. The issue wasn't *if* he would be able to do something; the questions were "how long will this take to master?" and "will I die trying?"

Besides the time in the ocean, these boys spent hundreds of hours on their 4-wheelers with Aaron leading the way in fearless abandon. Before you can understand what I mean by fearless abandon, you need

Living the South Florida life. Surf. Sand. Sun.

Aaron (2nd from left) with some of his new friends from our church

to understand that in Florida, vast areas of open land are not known as fields. They're much more sophisticated collections of mud. Here, they're called wetlands or preserves. And they do *not* exist for anyone's enjoyment. They exist for loftier purposes, and it's not taken lightly when a teenager has the audacity to utilize them for recreation of any kind. All of that means that any time the boys were 4-wheeling or mudding, they were looking out for the law.

Aaron saw this as a challenge—one he believed he could win.

Aaron's best friend Jason shared a story at the memorial service in Florida that had all of us rolling with laughter over one of their wetlands episodes. The way he told it, just around dusk one night, the woods suddenly lit up with headlights from a search team. The police had obviously been notified of the kids' presence in the wetland, which we affectionately referred to as "the holy land." Aaron, considering himself the SEAL-in-training, shouted for everyone to cut their engines and hide. (Jason explained that any time they went out, Aaron would come with a set of directions for routes of egress and a regroup station should they get split up while under pursuit.)

That night, Aaron left the others hiding behind a tree and belly-crawled into the darkness on a surveillance mission to see what challenges they faced should they be forced to make a run for it. In Jason's words: "Next thing I know, I hear leaves crunching and mud splashing. Here comes Aaron, blazing through the woods as fast as his legs could carry him. Never breaking stride, he mounts the 4-wheeler John Wayne style and screams, 'Run! They've got dawgs!'"

Always the leader, my boy was.

★

Over the years, Aaron and I developed a never-ending battle of trying to outdo each other with pranks. We both loved the sheer, childlike joy of pranking people.

I will admit that he absolutely bested me one day when I pulled up to a red light. We were in the far left of three lanes of traffic, and Aaron was in the passenger seat. Suddenly, I heard those famous words: "Hey Mom, watch this!"

Aaron proceeded to wad up a huge chunk of a napkin, stuff it in his mouth until it was completely saturated, whip the straw out of his soda, and shoot the spit wad onto the driver's window of an unsuspecting motorist two lanes over, navigating his shot between the cab and trailer of a semi in the middle lane. Just as the driver looked in our direction, Aaron threw himself to the floorboard, and I was left staring at a man who looked like he wanted to rip my head off as the slimy, wet paper slid down his driver-side window.

This was life with Aaron. And I loved every second of it.

He was a boy whose laughter could melt the hardest of hearts. It was so genuine…so hilarious. Even after he became a big, strong weapon of defense for the U.S. military, he would belly laugh like a child when something struck him as funny—mouth open, head thrown back, eyes squinted in pure hilarity. You couldn't help but laugh along.

That laugh—You just had to see it.

Chapter Eight

Broken Heart, Broken Dreams

For years, Aaron researched what it took to become a Navy SEAL. He learned that the Navy had developed a separate program for men who already knew they wanted to be SEALs—those who wanted to bypass regular Naval service and go directly to the Teams after enlisting. This process was called The SEAL Challenge Program.

The first step toward entering this famed program was the PST (Physical Screening Test). Aaron would need to be able to swim either breast-stroke or sidestroke for five hundred yards (five lengths of a football field) in twelve minutes and thirty seconds. Next, he would have to do at least fifty push-ups in two minutes, fifty sit-ups in the next two minutes, six pull-ups, and then run one-and-one-half miles—in boots and long pants in less than eleven minutes. These were the *minimum* requirements at that time. The expectations for unhindered advancement were much higher.

If Aaron passed the PST, he would continue on to Navy Boot Camp in Great Lakes, Illinois. After that, he would need to master Operations Specialist "A" School at Dam Neck Annex in Virginia Beach, Virginia. (Navy "A" School is an intense three-month long course on combat and command control systems.) After successful completion of both Boot Camp and Navy "A" School, he would be assigned a date to report to Coronado, California, for BUD/S (Basic Underwater Demolition/SEAL) Indoctrination. There he would be challenged with an even *more* intense PST before finally earning the privilege of joining the next BUD/S class.

During the summer before his senior year of high school, Aaron started testing himself to see just how challenging the PST would be. He trained like a madman day in and day out.

But, even with all his training, Aaron still managed to save plenty of time for fun—spitball wars at a local pizza place, surfing, flag football, concerts, beach time, and a whole lot of bonding. The summer between his junior and senior years was truly a summer to remember.

And then came fall.

Aaron's new Florida coaches had heard of his skills on the football field. They had seen the game tapes forwarded by his coaches in Tennessee and were more than anxious to put him to work. As practices began, Aaron's strengths became evident. So much so that his coach—who typically didn't allow players to work both sides of the line—made Aaron not only a wide receiver but also a defensive end. In the week leading up to the first game of his senior season, Aaron was asked to try his hand at defensive back (free safety). Aaron felt extremely honored by the opportunity and realized that things were falling into place. Since college football recruiting was much heavier in Florida than Tennessee, Aaron thought he might actually have the chance to receive a scholarship and play a little college football before entering the Navy.

On a Thursday afternoon, the day before the season opener, I arrived at the football stadium in time to catch the last hour of Aaron's practice. As soon as I reached the field, however, I quickly saw that something was very wrong. The entire team and all the coaches were huddled around a single player who was lying on the ground, writhing in pain.

Aaron.

My heart sank as I ran on to the field, everyone waving me in closer.

Aaron's coach met me halfway and said, "It's real bad, Mrs. Vaughn. It's his knee. You need to get him to the hospital."

After all the necessary medical tests were completed, we learned that Aaron had obliterated the Anterior Cruciate Ligament (ACL) in his left knee and had severely torn all three remaining ligaments. Surgery was the only option.

After a day or two of pretty serious depression, my boy came back like a lion. "I'll get the surgery. I'll get well. I can still play college ball. I can still do anything I put my mind to. This is mind over matter, Mom. I can beat this."

I had no doubt he was correct. Just like his encounter with White Cow all those years before, he was down, but he certainly wasn't out.

The ACL replacement surgery was seamless, and rehab went well. Once cleared for physical activity, Aaron was fitted for a special brace to support the injured joint, and the hard work of rebuilding his speed, strength, and agility began. He and I spent countless hours on the street in front of our home, working that knee with every contraption known to man. We used runner's parachutes, jumping shoes, speed shoes...you name it, we bought it. With tape marking off forty yards, I timed Aaron until he gained a consistent speed of 4.4–4.5 seconds, a remarkable time for a 6'4" man. Aaron had made a full, astonishing recovery, and his drive and tenacity blew everyone away.

With his senior football season a wash, Aaron's coaches did everything they could to get him that scholarship he had hoped for. Noting his courage, desire, and speed, colleges began sending letters. Interest had once again been piqued.

A few months before graduation, during an after school pick-up game of basketball, Aaron landed oddly and twisted his knee. At least, he thought he had twisted his knee. Tests revealed he had once again obliterated his ACL. Hopes for college football were over. And while that was a very hard reality to accept, Aaron still believed in his heart he could get the ligament replaced again, rehab as aggressively as he had before, and still be able to fulfill his *real* lifelong dream of becoming a SEAL.

But when his surgeon, one of the top orthopedics in the nation, went in for the second repair, he returned a few hours later with a life-shattering revelation. "There was nothing I could do. There was too much damage…nothing left of his knee to attach the new ACL to. I'm truly sorry."

The surgeon went on to explain that Aaron would spend the rest of his life somewhat handicapped and that he would never be able to participate in any physical activity again without the use of a special brace.

No words are capable of describing the loss Aaron experienced upon learning his new fate. Every dream he had ever dreamed, every vision of his future, every sacrifice solidified in sweat and blood…was over. As the anesthetic fog lifted, his devastating reality began to settle.

He would never be a Navy SEAL.

While grieving this tremendous loss with my son, I couldn't help but wonder why God had so radically denied Aaron the chance to live out the calling we all believed *He* had placed on Aaron's life. At the exact period of time when Aaron was preparing to spread his proverbial wings and fly off into his glorious destiny, he had instead been caged. It seemed like such a cruel twist of fate, but my faith that God still had a plan did not waiver. Nor did Aaron's.

We both knew that God's ways are higher than our ways. His plans are loftier than our own. One of Aaron's favorite verses in the Bible was Romans 8:28: "And we know that all things work together for good to those who love God, to those who are the called according to His purpose." (NKJV) We had learned to trust Him through many highs and lows and, therefore, had great confidence that whatever the future held would be for Aaron's good. We also knew that God certainly meant him no harm in what He had allowed to happen. However, trusting and claiming that verse still didn't make Aaron's new reality easy.

After a lifetime of believing he had been created for a monumental purpose, Aaron was now faced with the difficult task of resolving himself to a life of normalcy. His purpose was in question. He needed to find his *new* place in this world but had no idea where to begin looking. Something deep inside him changed in the days following the surgeon's news. The smallness of Aaron's once oversized grin reminded us constantly that he was struggling with the transition.

One afternoon he came home from school with an odd, kind of hesitant look on his face. I knew there was a "big ask" on its way.

"Mom, do you think I could go back to Tennessee for the last few weeks of school so I can graduate from Obion Central?"

Admittedly, I was taken aback by his request, but how on earth could I say no? He had spent almost his entire school career with his classmates from Obion County. I would have done anything to lift his spirits and give him something to look forward to.

"Wow...I guess...I mean I don't see why not."

"I could live with Daddy Frank and Nanu (those were the names Aaron had given my parents when he first learned to talk). They wouldn't mind."

"No, I'm sure they'd love that. I guess it's fine with me, but of course, I'll have to clear it with Dad...*and* both schools."

"Thanks, Mom. It would really mean a lot to me."

With little hesitation, Billy agreed, and within a couple of weeks, all the paperwork was completed. Aaron moved north, settled himself into one of my parents' spare bedrooms, and, quite honestly, had the time of his life. The fog of depression lifted, and his mental state improved. About six weeks later, Billy, Tara, Ana, and I traveled to Tennessee for Aaron's graduation. Even with all of the fun Aaron had had with his old friends, he was ready to return to Florida.

Shortly after moving home again, Aaron landed a job at an elite golf course on Jupiter Island, Florida. Because of his tremendous personality, impeccable work ethic, and can-do attitude, Jupiter Island Club offered Aaron a full scholarship to study golf course management at a local college. Aaron jumped at the invitation and embraced his new career with hope and excitement.

This was my first encounter with Aaron Vaughn, the student. The same child who had brought home less than stellar grades for most of his prior academic career suddenly brought home straight A's nearly every semester. Just like I had figured out years before, the question wasn't a matter of capability with Aaron, but instead a matter of logic—*Will this be important to me? If so, I'll give it my best shot. If not, get it out of my way.*

Academically, Aaron breezed through college and graduated with honors. However, he didn't bother walking for his diploma. Aaron lived and died by a creed so unfamiliar to most—he never wanted the attention of others. He didn't view his accomplishments as something to be celebrated or publicly acknowledged. He simply kept his head down, worked hard, and embraced the invaluable reward of personal satisfaction.

Chapter Nine

That Fateful Day

Aaron's life had settled into a pretty solid routine by the time he turned twenty. His job at the golf course suited him well, and he started making plans, with the help of his boss, to pursue a supervisory job. At the close of a typical workday, Aaron would spend time either surfing, fishing, or just horsing around with family and friends. He believed in having fun and making memories, and he was doing just that.

Little did Aaron and our entire family know how the events of 2001 would change us *and* our family's history.

★

In August of that year, my father, at age sixty-six, lost his four-year battle with cancer.

His death was a hard loss for our family. He fought valiantly, right up until the end. I had never seen anyone battle cancer with such dignity. His primary concern—through every setback—was making sure none of us worried. If he became uncomfortable, he would quietly dismiss himself to another room, making no fuss over the extreme pain he was experiencing. We all noticed him getting weaker, yet his spunk, love for life—and laughter—made it difficult to believe his journey was nearly over.

Dad and Aaron were a lot alike. Dad loved adventure, and perhaps

Aaron and Tara with my dad on the kids' first visit back to Tennessee after our move to Florida.

that's where Aaron inherited his adventurous spirit. Dad served in the US Army in the post-Korean War era, and Aaron deeply respected Dad's service. On a lighter note, Aaron also deeply respected the fact that my dad built a urinal into the wall of his garage, right beside his refrigerator full of beer. Aaron swore that one day when he built a home of his own he would do the same. He thought it was the coolest move ever. Dad and Aaron shared a lifelong admiration and love for each other. Aaron had that type of bond with each of his grandparents—unique individual relationships, but all with equal amounts of love.

In May 2001, Mom and Dad visited us in Florida for our daughter Tara's high school graduation. On one of the last days of their trip, Dad asked Aaron to take him mudding in his 4-wheel drive Jeep. Dad's spine was loaded with tumors at the time so Mom and I vehemently fought the idea. But Dad was determined to go. Maybe he knew in his heart this would be his last big outing with the boy he had loved so dearly for the past twenty years.

Dad crawled up into Aaron's Jeep and off they went to the "holy land," both of them grinning ear-to-ear. About an hour or so later, Billy, my mom, and I made a quick trip to the store. On our way back home, my mom—with a completely perplexed tone—interrupted our ongoing chitchat. "Hey, is that Rody?" (her nickname for my dad).

Billy threw on the brakes, made a quick U-turn, and drove back up the road to find Dad walking down the sidewalk toward the nearest service station. The two "boys" had buried the Jeep in mud, and Dad was headed out to get some help. Once we all regrouped, Dad and Aaron couldn't stop laughing about their escapade.

Two months later, we stood in a circle around Dad's hospital bed.

Watching him die.

My dad was a proud man and had spent a good deal of his life wavering in his faith. In his last few years, however, his faith in Christ solidified, and he knew exactly where he would go when he breathed his final breath.

Our entire family was blessed enough to be in the room to hear him say, "I see His face."

My mom rushed to his side, grasped both of his hands, and said, "Is it Jesus, honey?"

"Yes."

"Is He beautiful?"

"Yes."

And just like that, it was over.

Dad's heart didn't stop beating until three days later, but he never regained consciousness.

Aaron's heart broke.

We all broke.

We felt certain we had just endured the most unspeakably horrifying event any of us would ever witness.

We were wrong.

✦

Like any adult in America, I remember with great clarity every detail of my morning on September 11, 2001. I was working as a landscape designer in South Florida and had just stopped by one of my job sites to check on the crew. As I stepped out of the car, I could sense something was amiss. Our site supervisor headed toward me explaining nervously that a plane had struck one of the World Trade Center buildings where a sister of one of our crewmembers was working.

While that young man struggled to reach his sister and verify her safety, the rest of us attempted to understand how a plane could accidentally crash into the tower. It hadn't been reported yet that it was a passenger plane, so we all assumed it was a small, private aircraft. Maybe the pilot had a heart attack. Maybe he was intoxicated. Maybe he had simply lost control. We were curious and concerned as we continued sorting through blueprints while standing near our only source of news—a truck radio.

Ten minutes later we were *terrified*.

"Another plane has struck the second tower. (long pause) We can no longer consider this an accident. I believe we are witnessing a terror attack on the United States of America," explained the broadcaster.

It seemed as though—just for a moment—time stood still.

Finally composing ourselves, we all ran to our cars, flipped on our own radios, and began tracking down our loved ones.

By late afternoon, Billy and I and our three children sat huddled in our home in a complete state of shock. Glued to the news channels, we searched our minds for answers, trying to make sense of what we were witnessing—air traffic at a complete standstill for the first time in our lives; roads closed in and out of New York City; hopeless men and women jumping to their deaths as smoke billowed from windows behind them; replays of passenger planes striking the twin towers and the Pentagon; a downed airliner in a vacant field in Pennsylvania; ash-covered, bloodied men and women—terrified, dumbfounded, stunned— running frantically through the streets of lower Manhattan as the first, then the second, tower collapsed.

As these images of sheer horror flashed across the screen, an unspeakable anger flashed in my son's eyes—an intense and righteous anger that I immediately knew would not—could not—go unanswered.

As the sun began to set on that monstrous day, an intense, suffocating blanket of darkness covered our land, and without words, we all knew the "Shining City upon a Hill" would *never* be the same.

And there would be war.

"Freedom itself was attacked this morning by a faceless coward, and freedom will be defended… [The] United States will hunt down and punish those responsible for these cowardly acts." ~President George W. Bush from Barksdale Air Force Base.

★

In the following days, an astonishing story of bravery and sacrifice emerged: a story of common men and women with lions' hearts and a story that would inspire the nation and revive our crippled spirit. A story that rose from the ashes of a downed Boeing 757. Call sign: *Flight 93*.

In our home, we grieved as we listened to family members recount their frantic conversations of tender goodbyes and whispered words of "I love you," and "if I don't make its…." We heard the brave, awe-inspiring rumbles of courage—"It's happening!…It's up to us. I think we can do it."

Then finally, Todd Beamer's stoic battle cry which, in one instant, demolished, rebuilt, and refueled the heart of every patriot across this nation: "Let's roll."

The forty selfless heroes onboard Flight 93 didn't sit in their seats and pray that somehow their government would come to their rescue. They didn't bow in fear to a terrorist enemy determined to destroy them.

They acted.

Dressed in business suits and ties, blue jeans and t-shirts, these every-day Americans denied the terrorists their most fatal blow—a strike on our nation's capital. They would die so others could live.

There it was…that indomitable spirit of the America Aaron knew, the America he loved, the America of its founders who were willing to sacrifice their lives, their fortunes, and their sacred honor for this *dream* of a land where men could be free.

Todd Beamer's challenge would not go unanswered.

Months later, on Aaron's twenty-first birthday—June 24, 2002—he

The Navy recruiter snapped this Polaroid of Aaron on the day that he enlisted. He is dressed in his work clothes from the golf course, and shortly after this photo was taken, he came home to give us the news of his enlistment. This day was also Aaron's 21st birthday.

finished work on the plush golf course of Jupiter Island Club, and instead of coming directly home to the birthday dinner awaiting him, or making plans for a big night out with his buddies, he made a pit stop.

The United States Navy Recruiting Center.

When Aaron arrived home, his tone was deliberate, and his countenance somber. We knew he had something to tell us. As we sat down at the dinner table, the words finally left his lips.

"I joined the SEAL Challenge Program today. I leave for boot camp in November."

Silence.

Billy and I both struggled for the correct response.

After a few seconds, Billy spoke tenderly. "Son, how do you think you can make it through BUD/S with your knee?"

"I can do this, Dad. I know this is what I'm supposed to do."

Aaron was confident and unwavering.

I withdrew mentally as I began pondering the magnitude of what

Aaron had just done. My chest tightened with an odd fusion of pride and fear. While moved by his willingness to take his place in America's military history, this was no game. We were at war. US forces were dying as we spoke.

Billy's voice snapped me back to reality. "You do realize if you don't make it as a SEAL, you'll still be in the Navy, right?"

"I'll make it, Dad. I'm going to be a SEAL. I've *always* known it."

I deeply respected Aaron for his choice. And though my mother's heart wanted to shield him from harm, to demand he call and retract his signature, I knew it was pointless…and wrong.

If not Aaron, who? If not now, when?

A long-silenced call born in my son's heart many years earlier, a call known well by all who knew Aaron well, beckoned once again. And with the irrepressible character of every patriot whose bloodstained boots blazed the trails of freedom, Aaron answered that call with a resounding "Yes."

Billy and I truly honored and respected his desire to serve his nation, but we couldn't imagine how he planned to accomplish the overwhelming task he had placed before himself. With the condition of his left knee, his choice made no sense.

I remember asking, "Aaron, does the Navy know about your knee?"

His answer was almost comical. "Nooooo…they'd have never let me in."

Aaron then commenced to tell us that, unbeknownst to any of us, he had begun a training program shortly after the towers fell and was testing himself privately. He had done extensive research online to find exercises that would build muscle in order to stabilize the joint on its own. Over the previous three-plus years, he had worn a knee brace which, of course, would need to be left behind since its presence would betray his secret. If the Navy had known about his condition, his request to join the program would have been flat out denied.

On June 25, I once again became actively engaged in the knee

Aaron giving me a great big hug after Boot Camp graduation

rebuilding process. Aaron and I would have almost five months of working together until he left for boot camp, and his commitment to training and preparing was unparalleled. We spent countless hours online watching videos, reading article after article, and learning exactly what would be expected of him should he pass the early stages and make it to the famed land of Coronado, California, and the BUD/S training facility, where SEAL dreams are either shattered or fulfilled. His eyes would light up when he spoke about the possibility of one day crossing that two-mile-long suspension to greatness—the Coronado Bridge.

Before we could turn around twice, the day arrived. Aaron was leaving for boot camp. We loaded up the car after lunch on a Sunday afternoon and drove him to that same recruiter's office he had stopped by on his way home from work months earlier. We sat in the office, almost paralyzed. As silly jokes were made to lighten the mood, it was all white noise to me. My boy was leaving. I knew in my heart that if he achieved success, he would never be back. But how could I hope for anything different?

★

After having conditioned himself for SEAL Qualification Training,

Navy Boot Camp came and went with relatively little effort on Aaron's part. We attended the graduation ceremony in Great Lakes, Illinois, with hearts so full of pride that we thought they would explode.

Then came A-School in Virginia Beach. Billy and I visited Aaron during that portion of training, and together the three of us took our first trip to Washington, D.C. A massive protest was taking place that day at the Washington Monument making it very difficult to enjoy any of the prominent sites. However, our true interest lay at a place none of us had ever been, a place that rested on the other side of the Potomac—Arlington National Cemetery. As we entered the gates to Arlington, our eyes fell upon a now all-too-familiar sign and its sacred words.

Billy and Aaron on the day we visited Arlington National Cemetery together.

I struggled to breathe as I stood in awe, forced to look full in the face the sacrifices that had been made on my behalf. Row after row, field after field, line after line of white headstones. Billy, Aaron, and I walked those grounds for hours in silent reverence. We hardly spoke a word. It was one of the most memorable—and overwhelming—days of my entire life up to that point. Looking back now, I'm certain we walked on all four roads that now create the frame around Aaron's grave.

Part Two
The Warrior

Aaron in Iraq

Chapter Ten

BUD/S Class 248

IN LATE 2003, AARON'S NAME hit the roll for BUD/S Class 248. The phone call that followed was hilarious.

"Mom, I get to do a winter Hell Week! I can't believe it. This is so freaking awesome!"

"That's awesome, Son. Tell me, though…why is it, exactly, *awesome* that you're doing it in the winter? That doesn't sound like a good thing?"

"Because then everyone knows you didn't just make it. You made it under the *worst* conditions. *Everyone* wants to say they had a winter Hell Week. I mean, the water is like in the 40s and 50s, and so you're not just wet, you're wet and freezing all the time! There's a huge dropout rate."

I couldn't help but laugh. Like the knee wasn't going to be challenging enough? He needed the harshest weather conditions as well? I loved his spirit so much.

Before the long-awaited trip to Coronado, the Navy provided Aaron a brief trip home to celebrate with family and friends and to say goodbye. I remember finding it very difficult to control the battle raging in my heart. At his send-off party, I would look across the room periodically and see this grown man where my little boy should have been. I would smile with pride as I watched his buddies slap him on the back and laugh about who knows what, but at the same time, my heart felt as though it would explode from the pressure of knowing how radically life was about to change.

Aaron had been there from the beginning. For twenty-two years I had not known a day without Aaron in it. I couldn't imagine life without him. It was surreal. The next morning he would begin his 2,500-mile trip to glory—to legendary status—should he succeed.

By this time, little doubt was left in my heart that Aaron would make it. He had been created for this moment. He had always known his destiny. And while circumstances had interfered with *his* plans, they had had no effect on God's.

Early the next morning, we woke up and loaded the Jeep Wrangler. Billy and Aaron checked the oil, jiggled the battery cables, and then slammed the hood. The sound shook me. It was time. My baby was really leaving. Wiping my eyes, I regained my composure and snapped a picture as Aaron, with a huge smile plastered on his face, hugged his dad goodbye, and then I took another as he backed out of our driveway.

I spent the next months in what seemed like constant prayer.

BUD/S is a six-month intensive training course with Hell Week occurring at the four-week mark. For all those who survive Hell Week, a brown shirt lies on the shoreline—last name stenciled on the chest. Once you earn the right to a brown shirt, you've turned a significant corner and will most likely, at some point, make it into the Teams.

Near midnight one December evening, our phone rang.

"I got my brown shirt."

But Aaron's words weren't enunciated that clearly. Because his tongue was so swollen from dehydration, he had to repeat the phrase three or four times before I realized what he had said. Emotion overcame me, and all I could do was cry. I broke down.

"I'm so proud of you, Son. I am so incredibly proud of you."

Then Billy started crying.

Billy and I looked at each other in total disbelief. This had actually

The last hug before Aaron headed off to Coronado for the very first time.

Sheer determination— A BUD/S instructor took this photo of Aaron.

happened. Aaron was going to be a Navy SEAL. All those hopes, all that hard work, and all that belief in God had paid off. Our boy would live his dream.

In an unexpected act of kindness from the hands of his BUD/S instructors, Aaron received permission to come home immediately following Hell Week to participate in his sister Tara's wedding. While his trip was quick, its value was immeasurable. Every word he uttered throughout that weekend had our full attention. His heart was still racing with excitement over what he had just survived.

He struggled as he tried to help us envision what Hell Week had been like. Just after sundown on a Sunday, Hell Week began with a hair-raising Normandy Beach-like scenario of absolute chaos: their doors kicked open by instructors firing weapons (loaded with blanks, of course), artillery simulators blasting, and loud whistles and bellowed commands piercing their ears.

The men were then forced outside where even greater chaos ensued. They were knocked to the ground with high-powered water jets while gunfire, explosions, commands, and screeching whistle blows continued. My mind reeled trying to imagine in some small way what it must have been like. As Aaron spoke, we could almost hear the deafening rounds and smell the cordite.

And that was just the first few minutes of a hellacious event that would continue for another five days and nights. Unimaginably, in that roughly 120-hour block of constant physical and mental stress, Aaron and the other men had only four hours of sleep. Total.

We cringed through the stories of overcoming hour upon hour in a near-freezing ocean where body cavity temperature checks were as much a part of survival as the few and far between periods of rest. As if the freezing surf wasn't torture enough, the would-be warriors were repeatedly forced to dip their frozen, sand-covered bodies in horse troughs full of iced water. We physically ached as we looked at all the areas of raw flesh on Aaron's body brought about from a constant covering of sand grating against his skin through every exercise, every movement. We also noticed large chunks of hair missing from his scalp. This, we learned, came from hours of running with a 110-pound inflatable boat overhead pounding his skull with every footfall.

We laughed together as Aaron told about some of his more light-hearted memories.

"I'm tellin' you…it was crazy. I mean you never sleep. Just like fifteen minutes at a time here and there. So your head is just messed up all the time." Then laughing out loud, eyes squinted in hilarity while picturing the memory, he continued, "I even hallucinated a couple times. One morning I looked down in my cereal bowl, and I swear, I saw the cowardly lion off 'The Wizard of Oz' staring up at me, laughing and, like, mocking me!"

My eyes welled with tears, though, as he described the final moments of Hell Week.

"It's just craziness and chaos. You don't know what time it is, and you're not really sure what day it is. So you don't have any idea how much longer it's gonna last. The instructors had us lock arms and face the water, and we all thought it was gonna be just another round of surf torture. Then all of a sudden someone told us to turn around and there, stretched out across the berm, was every one of our instructors. One of them was holding an American flag. Our brown shirts were laying in the sand right there in front of them with our names stenciled on the chest, and we knew it. It was over." His voice shifted to a more serious tone as his mind went back to the moment, and he almost choked up as the words left his mouth. "Then our commander shouted, 'Hell Week is secured.'"

It was over.

Aaron's body was ravaged, but his spirit screamed with satisfaction, pride, and confidence. You could see it in his eyes. Never again would he face a challenge too great to overcome. He had experienced firsthand the true meaning of the gospel he had read so many times—"I can do all things through Christ, Who gives me strength." (Philippians 4:13)

Many have asked where Aaron's tenacity came from to endure and conquer such insurmountable obstacles. While his faith in God's call on his life was unshakeable, I'm certain the principles we taught him throughout his childhood and young adult years played a significant role. While Billy and I oftentimes had different approaches to teaching our kids, we worked together to teach them the importance of properly handling success and failure. I tended to be my children's greatest cheerleader and wanted to instill in them that they could accomplish anything they put their minds to, while Billy's focus was more on helping our children see and understand areas of their lives and character where they could improve.

Children need a balance of praise and criticism in order to develop a healthy self-worth. We can't praise them when they're doing something poorly and expect them to give more or try harder the next time. We need to teach them that failure is real and entirely possible, but we also need to teach them that failure is not final and that they can accomplish great things. The purpose of allowing failure is to build character and teach that anything worth having requires effort. We allowed Aaron to fail which made his moments of success all that much sweeter in his eyes.

One of the other concepts we instilled in our children was "you don't quit until the whistle blows." Remember the star quarterback that Aaron kept blasting back in high school? That was a perfect example. It's fine that he had to be called off. At least everyone on that team knew Aaron could be trusted to give it his all, all the time. His teammates respected him for that. We also taught them "when the going gets tough, the tough get going." You don't cry when you want to quit. You push and push and push until you feel like you've given *more* than you had in you. Only then will you realize what you're truly capable of achieving.

★

As perfect as Tara's wedding weekend was, it was over in a flash. And we were saying goodbye.

Again.

Aaron returned to Coronado to complete Phase One and the remaining months of his training. Many fall by the wayside in the second leg—Dive Phase—where men are pushed past all reasonable limits in underwater survival. But Aaron sailed through. I attribute his success in Dive Phase to our move to Florida and his endless hours in the surf and learning not to panic when a wave held him under. With undeviating calculation, God had prepared Aaron for everything. The fight and endurance he cultivated to overcome his knee injury gave him the confidence and determination he needed to get through Phase One. The surfer years in sunny South Florida shoved him through Phase Two. Then came Phase Three: Land Warfare. If his childhood hadn't prepared him for that, nothing would have. He knew weapons, he had fast-roped down hundreds of vines, he had blown things up, and he had found his way out of the woods by the position of the sun so many times he could

Granny (Billy's mom), Aaron, and Nanu (my mom) just before Tara's wedding.

Cousins at Tara's wedding—(left to right) Ashleigh, Courtney, Tara, Aaron, Trey, Garrett.

Aaron had a lot of experience with face painting, a skill that he had honed on our farm in Tennessee.

BUD/S Graduation—What an amazing day!

do it with his eyes shut. All those skills had been developed on the training ground of our small farm back home in the land of cotton and Big Orange football. Phase Three was nearly effortless.

★

On April 30, 2004, our family arrived at The Grinder—the large concrete/asphalt testing ground where giants are made or men are broken—and proudly watched as Aaron took his place as one of the few in history who had successfully completed BUD/S training. He had overcome unimaginable odds to secure his place in history, to be named among the elite, to be called a US Navy SEAL.

His class, which had started with around 160 men, finished with less than ten of those originals. Helmets of all those who had "Rung Out," who had given up short of reaching the goal, lined The Grinder that day. When a man has reached his limit, he removes his helmet, lays it down, and tugs the rope of a huge brass bell that hangs on the edge of this paved square of victory or defeat. This is an act of no return.

During one of our conversations, Aaron explained to me that in order to become a Navy SEAL you have to want it so badly that you're willing to die for it. And if you *should* actually stop breathing, you then have to be willing to trust those around you enough to know they'll resuscitate you. If you can put your life in their hands and release your welfare and safety to them completely, then—and only then—can you earn the title "Frogman"…Team Guy.

★

I believe there's great beauty in the fact that God sees our entire story—start to finish—and patiently allows us to be confounded and even sometimes angered by our own lack of vision. Because of His mercy, He lovingly utilizes our weakness to expose His greatness, and in so doing, builds our faith…our trust…our hope.

Such was the case with Aaron's irreparable knee injury.

Though I've never seen it, I've been told Aaron's name is on a self-descriptive plaque at the BUD/S compound in Coronado titled "First Time

Every Time." Aaron, with no ACL in his left knee, completed every evolution required of him on his first attempt.

By becoming a Navy SEAL, and ultimately rising all the way to SEAL Team VI, Aaron accomplished the near-impossible. There was only one plausible explanation:

God.

God had been there every moment, and Aaron never took that for granted. He never beat his chest and said, "Look what *I* did!" Instead, I very often heard him say, in complete humility, "I can't believe God has let me do this." He was always quick to point all the glory and all the praise to His creator and sustainer, Jesus Christ.

Our warrior was now fully trained and ready.

Chapter Eleven

A Creed to Live By

The SEAL Ethos

In times of war or uncertainty there is a special breed of warrior ready to answer our Nation's call. A common man with uncommon desire to succeed. Forged by adversity, he stands alongside America's finest special operations forces to serve his country, the American people, and protect their way of life. I am that man.

My Trident is a symbol of honor and heritage. Bestowed upon me by the heroes that have gone before, it embodies the trust of those I have sworn to protect. By wearing the Trident I accept the responsibility of my chosen profession and way of life. It is a privilege that I must earn every day.

My loyalty to Country and Team is beyond reproach. I humbly serve as a guardian to my fellow Americans always ready to defend those who are unable to defend themselves. I do not advertise the nature of my work, nor seek recognition for my actions. I voluntarily accept the inherent hazards of my profession, placing the welfare and security of others before my own.

I serve with honor on and off the battlefield. The ability to control my emotions and my actions, regardless of circumstance, sets me apart from other men. Uncompromising integrity is my standard. My character and honor are steadfast. My word is my bond.

We expect to lead and be led. In the absence of orders I will take charge, lead my teammates and accomplish the mission. I lead by example in all situations.

I will never quit. I persevere and thrive on adversity. My Nation expects me to be physically harder and mentally stronger than my enemies. If knocked down, I will get back up, every time. I will draw on every remaining ounce of strength to protect my teammates and to accomplish our mission. I am never out of the fight.

We demand discipline. We expect innovation. The lives of my teammates and the success of our mission depend on me - my technical skill, tactical proficiency, and attention to detail. My training is never complete.

We train for war and fight to win. I stand ready to bring the full spectrum of combat power to bear in order to achieve my mission and the goals established by my country. The execution of my duties will be swift and violent when required yet guided by the very principles that I serve to defend.

Brave men have fought and died building the proud tradition and feared reputation that I am bound to uphold. In the worst of conditions, the legacy of my teammates steadies my resolve and silently guides my every deed. I will not fail.

AFTER BUD/S, AARON, LIKE ALL those who went before him, endured six additional months of rigorous, exhaustive SEAL Qualification Training before the day came when he finally recited the SEAL Ethos and received his long-sought-after SEAL Trident.

The Trident is a unique Special Warfare pin. All SEALS, whether officers or enlisted men, wear the same pin. No variation whatsoever. The identical pins are a reflection on how these men train together and fight together, and no man is greater than the other. They take it to the enemy as equals—a brotherhood—with virtually no distinction.

The Trident is comprised of a golden eagle clutching a U.S. Navy anchor, Neptune's spear, and a flintlock pistol. Each portion of this emblem reflects the SEAL's character, work ethic, and skill set.

The day Aaron earned his Trident. He is pictured with Michael Tatham who is also no longer with us on earth.

The anchor symbolizes the SEAL's parent service, the Navy. On closer inspection, one will notice an inscription on the anchor—a date from times past. SEALs are taught to honor and guard the legacy handed down to them by the heroes who've gone before. They take great pride in their roots—the Naval Combat Demolition Units and Underwater Demolition Teams.

In the eagle's right claw is Neptune's spear. Historically, the right hand signifies power, and Neptune was the ancient Roman god of the sea. This is a representation of a SEAL's most noted skillset: their uncanny ability to operate underwater. By the time a man is pinned with the Trident, he's as at home beneath the sea as he is on land.

The pistol, gripped by the eagle's left claw, signifies that SEALs are equally trained in land combat. It's important to note that the pistol is cocked and ready to fire. This is the life of a Navy SEAL…ready to go—ready to fight—at a moment's notice, always prepared when called upon by their nation, and never caught off-guard.

The eagle, our nation's symbol of freedom, indicates the SEAL's ability to insert from the air. It also characterizes their core standards: bravery, swiftness, and honor. On most military insignias you'll find an eagle's head held high, but not so on the Trident. On this badge of honor, the eagle's head is bowed low. While the eagle carries out its missions on land, in the air, and in the sea, it does so with great humility. No need for accolades. No desire for attention.

★

If you think for a second that a SEAL is a breed of warrior with an ounce of arrogance regarding his accomplishments, you're mistaken. These men are sifted through a complex series of mental evaluations. Those lacking the character necessary to represent the tradition of integrity and humility solidified in the SEAL community are quickly and easily weeded out. You would be hard-pressed to ever hear one of them declare their line of work in a public *or* private setting. If you happen to hear someone state they are a SEAL, you should immediately suspect whether or not his tale is true.

Aaron exemplified this humility. If asked, he would never declare his occupation to be anything grander than "I'm in the military." That statement was sufficient for him. There were no celebratory homecomings when he returned from war—no flags waving, no touching kisses or hugs caught on camera. As a matter of fact, he usually arrived at the airport in blue jeans, a Tennessee VOLS ball cap, and one of his favorite T-shirts that said something ridiculous like "More Cowbell" or "Paper Football Champions, Class of 1982." He would come and go in total obscurity and was more than content doing so.

I have to admit that his humility and desire for obscurity was tough for me to watch. I wanted the world to know where he had been, how courageously he had defended us, and how amazing he was.

But, silence was the creed.

I remember on one occasion visiting Aaron in his hometown of Coronado and experiencing the full wrath of dishonoring the creed. Two young men sitting near us in a crowded restaurant started boasting about being in BUD/S, giving loud-mouth, colorful descriptions of some of the situations—and instructors—they had encountered. They were seeking attention, and, boy, were they about to get it.

Billy and I glanced at each other because we both noticed the obvious tension and shift in Aaron's demeanor. He disengaged from the conversation at our table and laser-focused on the one taking place at the next. Right in the middle of one of Billy's sentences, Aaron shoved himself up from his chair, slammed his fist on the table—rattling our plates and glasses—and unloaded on the two young men.

"Shut your (expletive) mouths! Who do you think you are and what do you think you're doing? Get your (expletive) out of here and don't ever let me see your faces again. You disgust me. Shut your stupid mouths and get out!"

In nearly unintelligible whispers, they replied, "Yes, sir. We're sorry, sir." And dismissed themselves.

I'm pretty confident that their attempt at making it into the Teams was finished. Aaron wouldn't forget their faces.

Shifting back to his gentle demeanor, Aaron turned to us and simply said, "I'm sorry."

No apology was necessary. We understood.

Yes, the eagle's head is bowed low on the coveted Trident. A raised and proud head draws attention. A bowed head works and achieves with no accolades required or requested.

But don't mistake the humility and determination of a SEAL and his teammates as an inability to have fun and take full advantage of the circumstances surrounding them. These men live.

They live large.

When they're working, no one works harder. Likewise, when they're playing, few play harder. Laughter keeps them balanced. And, they all seem to be drawn to extreme adventure, living to tell some pretty fascinating stories.

Aaron took up dirt bike riding as his form of release. I'll probably never know the full extent of what happened one particular day, but I do know it started with a "Hey y'all, watch this" jump in the Baja Desert. It ended at the hospital emergency room with a concussion and a few

The boy loved anything with wheels.

fractures, including a fractured scapula, an injury I understand as very difficult to acquire. Since these men are so highly trained and invested in by our military, Aaron was respectfully asked to retire the bike and take up safer forms of recreation. I'm not certain he ever fully complied.

Because Navy SEALs get to hone their skills at the top training facilities around the world, Aaron often came home with entertaining stories. They flipped 4-wheelers down mountainous terrains, wrecked cars, flipped golf carts, and on and on the stories went. It seemed like they destroyed everything they laid their hands on. At times they were even *challenged* to see how much it took to destroy a new piece of equipment that was still in its trial phase. While the stories were great, the problem came when Aaron visited us and treated his father's things the same way. Oh boy, did we ever get some laughs watching Billy try to reign in his great big, grown, Navy SEAL son!

When Aaron sat on our 4-wheeler, he was no longer content to just *ride* it like during his teen years. He had to see how far he could wind out the engine or how much of the driveway he could jump. On his very

Aaron scaling the side of a ship. Not an easy task!

last trip home to South Florida, he and his dad took our new boat out. Within minutes, it was totally grounded—engines wide open, Aaron laughing hysterically.

As Billy puts it—"The boy was hard on stuff."

When Aaron drove my car, we literally slid sideways around corners—me hanging on for dear life—until finally skidding to a halt in our driveway. Aaron would be instructing me the entire time on "defensive driving skills," as if one day I would need to know how to bump the back end of another car in order to fling it off the road in a tailspin! I was doing everything in my power to just hold my lunch down much less learn anything. But, man, did we ever laugh.

I'll never forget the day Aaron, always the prankster, laid rubber in an elementary school parking lot in MY CAR. He cracked up because he knew everyone would think it was me behind the wheel. That antic honestly got me riled, which, of course, made it all the more funny to him.

Oh, he was crazy fun…and funny.

One night we were having one of our serious mom/son talks, discussing tender topics about faith and family and such. Something I had been thinking about for a long time suddenly surfaced. In complete sincerity, I looked at Aaron and said, "Son, I know you're doing what you were called to do, but something has been really confusing to me. When you were young, I always believed God was telling me that one day you'd be a great missionary. I just don't get how I could have been so wrong."

With his unbelievably quick wit, he laughed and said, "Well, Mom... maybe you just didn't hear Him right. Maybe He was trying to tell you I'd be a great mercenary!"

On another one of his trips home, Aaron decided that Ana, his baby sister, twelve years his junior, should become a cage fighter. A *cage fighter*! Being possibly the most fearless of all three of our children, Ana definitely had what it took. Although she was only thirteen years old at the time, having her big brother speak this into her heart made her believe she wanted it too. On and on it went, day after day. Almost every time I walked through the house, the two of them would be on our bedroom floor (the only room in the house with carpet) twisted in pretzel-like positions, working on her new skill set. She stuck with Aaron for hours at a time.

One morning I walked into Ana's room before she woke up. I found her on a heating pad, nursing her aching body, with a bottle of pain relievers lying on the floor. When she realized I had discovered her secret, she begged me not to tell Aaron because she was afraid it would make him go easy on her. Of course, I told him. Thankfully, that trip was the only time we heard about Ana's desire to be a cage fighter. However, her cage fighting training days gave us a source of laughter for many years.

Aaron was extreme in every way: extremely fierce, extremely gifted, extremely humble, extremely kind, and extremely encouraging. Any time you were in his presence, you felt you could conquer the world. He believed in people, and people were better—and more courageous—for having known him.

Chapter Twelve

A Stroke of Love Called You

WHILE AARON EMBRACED ALL THE good in his riotous new life of extravagant adventure, something was still missing, something he had not attained.

Love.

Aaron had always been a man who loved the idea of love; he had just never known it. He had been in a few relationships, but each ended poorly. Even in high school, Aaron never dated for the sake of dating. He was no ladies' man. He was on the lookout for a soul mate, an enduring love, and, in return, he received nothing but letdowns.

One day, after finalizing a pretty painful breakup with someone he had been dating for a while, he called home for a good long, mom/son heart-to-heart. During that conversation, he said something I'll never forget. (Since Aaron's death, I've shared the following in a playful manner, but at the time nothing was funny about it.)

"Mom, there's only one thing in this world I'm afraid of, and that's women. I don't think there's another thing on earth that could honestly hurt me, but *they* sure can."

Aaron saw his desire for a committed relationship as a danger zone, and my heart broke as he told himself it would be healthier to just quit trying. I tried to encourage him.

"Son, there's someone out there for each of us, and every relationship prior to meeting that special someone will, by the grace of God, fail…if we're fortunate. You need to try seeing this as a blessing. The right one is waiting for you, and you *will* find her."

And find her he did.

★

God has a way of timing things that leaves no question as to whether or not He was involved in the unfolding of the events. In late 2005, Aaron was deployed in the Pacific Theatre and, at one point, did a short stint in Guam. While he was there, a group of Washington Redskins Cheerleaders flew in during a leg of their Armed Forces Entertainment Tour. After their last show, the cheerleaders visited a local hangout, and it was there in that crowded tavern, thousands of miles from home, paths crossed and a story of love began. Kimberly spotted Aaron across the room and made her way to him. The rest, as they say, is history.

Here's an excerpt from an email Aaron sent me in early 2006:

I honestly believe she's the one. We are crazy about each other. I'm hon-estly happier about her than I ever have been with any girl. She's amazing. Exactly what I've always been looking for. You'll love her. The things she wants are the same things I want, right down to God being number one in your spouse's life. It's amazing. Well, I gotta go. Hopefully, I can call soon. I love y'all.
Talk to you later,
Aaron

★

Later that year, Billy and I decided that our Christmas gift to each of our children would be an all-expense-paid vacation to New York City for New Years' Eve. We included Kimberly as well since she and Aaron were, by this time, in a very serious relationship. Aaron came home for a visit a few months before Christmas, and while here, he and Tara designed and ordered what Aaron called "*THE* Kimberly Linberger Engagement Ring."

It was huge.

The ring was scheduled to be ready by the time Aaron returned home in December. As you can imagine, we spent hours talking about awesome, memorable ways to propose. The moment had to be big.

When Aaron opened his present on Christmas morning and found the tickets to New York City, his eyes lit up. Before he could speak, we *all* knew what he was thinking. He and his sisters raced to the mall the next day so he could find "the perfect shirt and cologne" to propose in. He was a hopeless romantic!

A week later on New Year's Eve, Kimberly was the only one in our family watching the ball drop in Times Square. The rest of us were standing ready, cameras in hand. As the massive crowd descended the count, 5-4-3-2-1, Kimberly spun around to kiss Aaron, but he was down on one knee—ring in hand—grinning from ear to ear. Her reaction was priceless and just what he had hoped for.

Moments after Aaron popped the question

I will treasure that memory forever. I believe many times in life we take the real joy and full measure of a moment for granted, but this was not one of those times. Aaron and Kimberly had built and maintained a relationship while living on opposite coasts of our country. Now, they would finally be together. They would finally be one. Our son had found love, and that love was reciprocated.

She said "yes."

In that split second, *everything* was as it should be. All was well, and we were happy. Our family was about to grow again.

✳

The wedding plans began, but the date was postponed longer than anyone wanted because Aaron was deploying to Afghanistan again. Before his deployment started, he came home for a good, long visit and brought Kimberly along.

I distinctly remember their last night in our home before heading back to Coronado where Aaron would ship off from. Our entire family gathered for dinner, and as Billy said the blessing, he spent quite a bit of time praying for Aaron's safety through the dangerous months ahead. At that point, a strange thing happened—

Kimberly began crying. And I fell apart.

Not because Aaron was leaving. He had left many times before, and I was accustomed to shoving *those* tears to the back of my heart. I fell apart because for the first time in his life someone besides us loved him enough to worry about him, to cry for him, to long for his return. Kimberly's tears were ribbons of beauty caressing my soul. There it was… my son was loved. And he was loved *deeply*.

Aaron and Kimberly at our home before Aaron's deployment

The time had now arrived for us to let go of Aaron in a whole new way. The Bible says, "Therefore shall a man leave his father and his mother, and shall cleave unto his wife: and they shall be one flesh." God's Word references that verse at least four different times, and if I've learned anything from studying His Word, it's this—when God says something, He means it, but when He sees fit to repeat it multiple times, you better pay attention!

Over the years, I had seen marriages completely destroyed by parents who would not get out of the way, and Billy and I were determined to *never* be those parents. In some strange yet comforting way, my grip loosened almost instinctively. My labor of love—raising Aaron—was complete. And since almost every young wife sees her new husband as a work in progress, ready to be molded into the next phase of perfection, I was pretty comfortable handing that continuing education over to Kimberly.

My work was done.

Aaron and Kimberly's engagement photo

Chapter Thirteen

The Big Day

GOD BLESSED AARON BEYOND HIS wildest imagination when Kimberly walked into his life. Both Aaron and Kimberly had waited patiently for real love and endured painful ups and downs, crushed expectations, and multiple broken hearts before finding each other.

During one of their visits to Florida before the wedding, I played an old song for them—one *I* thought would be *perfect* for their big day: Larry Graham's "One In A Million You."

As the oldie but goodie (from 1980) bellowed out of my laptop speakers, I closed my eyes and envisioned them dancing their first dance as man and wife, looking over to me with gratitude for sharing this epic song with them. I just knew the lyrics were moving them the way they were moving me. When I finally turned to see their reaction to the song, they were struggling to not burst out laughing.

"We like the words, Mom. But it's *really* old-fashioned. I think we're gonna keep looking."

And they found the perfect song: "The Story" by Brandi Carlile. I had never heard the song before, but it couldn't have been more fitting for the two of them. I was glad they had continued their search and did not indulge me by agreeing to my selection.

Enjoying Capitol Hill the day before the wedding—
(left to right) Annabelle, Ana, me, Aaron, Tara, and Adam

Kimberly and Aaron set their big day for Saturday, May 3, 2008. But on May 1st, they were hit squarely in the face with the unpredictable reality of military life.

Earlier that week, Aaron had packed up everything he owned, left Coronado, and headed across the country to Virginia Beach, where he was scheduled to begin training and evaluation for the famed DEVGRU (Development Group), better known as SEAL Team VI. Since Aaron had first dreamed of becoming a Navy SEAL, this illusive Tier I Operations Command was his ultimate goal. Aaron's move to the East Coast was made even better by the fact that Kimberly had grown up in the Northern Virginia area and the relocation would allow her to be close to her family whenever Aaron deployed.

On the Thursday before the wedding, Kimberly busied herself with last-minute wedding preparations while Aaron showed us around Washington, D.C. Part way through our day, Aaron's phone rang, and within seconds of answering, his countenance dropped. Serious stress changed the pallor of his face. We didn't know what to expect when he hung up the phone, but we had overheard enough of the conversation to know

*Cousins Ethan, Trey, and Aaron in D.C. Aaron is on the phone
attempting to change his orders to return to Coronado.*

that he was speaking with his commander in California.

"I have to go back…(long pause)…They want me to be an instructor at Coronado for at least *two* years."

"Oh no, Son!"

"Yeah, they said there's been some incidents lately, and because of that, the training staff has to be increased."

Billy tried to offer words of encouragement, "Son, you know—"

"I know, Dad." Aaron interrupted. "I've gotta trust it's what God wants for me, and it's for a good reason."

We could see the stress and disappointment in his eyes. He spent the next hour or so—and a large part of the next day—making calls to see if anything could be done…if anything could be shifted…but to no avail.

Although the relocation would be a tremendous setback to Aaron's goals and dreams, his greatest concern was Kimberly and how the news would affect her. He was afraid it would strip the joy from their big day, but Kimberly was incredible. She took the hit in stride and began reassuring *Aaron* that everything would be fine. I loved how she embraced the change and encouraged my son.

Aaron in awe that this woman is his wife.
He looks so happy!

So, on Saturday, Aaron and Kimberly married as planned. They spent the next day or two celebrating as newlyweds and then packed up Aaron's truck once again. Brad Cavner—Aaron's best friend, fellow SEAL, and a best man in his wedding—joined Aaron on the long, nearly three-thousand-mile trip straight back to Coronado. Kimberly followed after packing up her home and notifying her workplace of the change in plans. Our boy had most assuredly found the right woman for the life that lay ahead.

✫

For the rehearsal dinner, I had created a video using their song "The Story" and a host of photos from the previous two years. Before the first picture appeared, the following quote from *The Wonder Years* scrolled on the screen:

All our young lives we search for someone to love.
Someone who makes us complete.
We choose partners and change partners.
We dance to a song of heartbreak and hope.
All the while wondering if somewhere, somehow,
there's someone perfect who might be searching for us.

Everything about their story was perfect…except the ending.

Chapter Fourteen

All in God's Plan

So many times throughout life I've been able to look back and see that what *seemed* to be a setback of some sort was actually a protective and loving act of God. Aaron's retraction to the West Coast training facility days before his wedding for the following two years was exactly that—the faithful hand of his loving God.

While Navy SEALS operate at a demanding level with never-ending training, travel, and deployments, DEVGRU operates at an even more intense pace. Had Aaron gone straight to DEVGRU after the wedding, he and Kimberly would have had almost no time to grow together as a couple. Now, since he was based at the training facility, Aaron worked what was basically a nine-to-five schedule with intermittent travel—and one six-month deployment. We all began to see how God gave Aaron and Kimberly those two years in Coronado to solidify their marriage, start their family, and spend not only quality time together, but also large quantities of time.

In September 2009 Aaron and Kimberly welcomed their first child into the world—Reagan Carson Vaughn. He had a big name to live up to, but he also had just the parents to make sure it would be accomplished. Nothing was as beautiful as the way Aaron looked at that little boy. Aaron's world had been made whole.

Aaron holding Reagan's tiny hand while sleeping

Life was good.

Just before Reagan's birth, Aaron was approached by military leaders and asked to help film a motion picture described to him as the US Navy SEAL equivalent to *Top Gun*. The film would be used as a recruitment tool to stir interest in becoming a special operator. By this time our country had been at war for eight years and reinforcements weren't coming in fast enough. Aaron agreed and took his spot in history in the now-famous movie *Act of Valor* (which didn't hit theaters until after his death). Because he was in Coronado at the right time—God's time—Aaron's children now have footage of their bigger-than-life, hero father authentically working as a Navy SEAL. For this, I am eternally grateful.

Then in late 2009, Aaron temporarily left his trainer position at Coronado to deploy for the first time with the Team he had dreamed of being a part of since he was a little boy. He was heading to Afghanistan with DEVGRU, also known as SEAL Team VI. (Aaron had not yet undergone the official training for DEVGRU—that was to come—but he was chosen to work with them for this deployment). To say he was stoked would be an understatement. To say we were stoked would be the exact opposite. Now that he had a wife and child counting on his safe return, deployments felt much more ominous.

And war was changing my son.

I noticed more and more that Aaron watched in silence as the rest of us laughed and engaged each other with reckless abandon, the kind of abandon he used to be the master of. Oh, don't get me wrong, he would seize opportunities here and there to cut loose and be himself, but the old, light-hearted Aaron was gone…and understandably so.

I can't imagine how surreal it must have been for Aaron to leave a battlefield where his life and the lives of his buddies were under constant threat only to come home to a nation of sheep oblivious to the fact that anyone was sacrificing anything on their behalves.

Many times, as an offering of encouragement, I sent Aaron Bible verses about King David's mighty men of valor and the love he had for them until the day he died. I reminded Aaron that David's final words were offerings of praise to those who stood beside him in the theater of battle, proving God always honored the hard and thankless work of a righteous warrior.

While Aaron had no questions about the purpose of the work he had been called to, he *did*, from time to time, need reassurance that his mother understood. In the most tender of moments, I would sense him searching for my absolution, needing to know I was not shocked or disheartened by the *real* work of his calling. At times, he would describe carefully chosen bits and pieces of a mission while never losing eye contact with me. I knew he was probably anticipating an adverse reaction on my part, but there was none. Ever. I always made sure that in my eyes Aaron only saw confidence and undaunted support.

When Aaron and Billy entered deeper, more difficult conversations, I would often leave the room, not for *my* peace of mind, but for Aaron's. There were things I didn't need to know, things I didn't want him to have to share in my presence.

War is ugly. It's real. It's not a motion picture or video game, and it's certainly not for the faint of heart. Real people die gruesome, horrible deaths, and in battle you either kill or *you* are killed. Billy and I always made sure Aaron knew we would never question a decision he made in battle and that his righteous heart could always be trusted. He'll never know how deeply I respected him for the hard life he chose.

Aaron and a teammate in the Hindu Kush Mountains of Afghanistan

Chapter Fifteen

Life as a SEAL

G OD REACHED OUT TO ME many times while Aaron was deployed, giving me comfort through dreams or words spoken that only He and I understood the significance of.

On one particular occasion, I dreamed in the most vivid, life-like setting imaginable that I was in our old farmhouse back in Tennessee. Walking into the utility room in the back of our home, I glanced out the window and noticed something move in the darkness. The object ducked behind the huge oak tree we used to picnic under when Aaron was a child. The tree stood near an old shed on the edge of the lawn, just this side of the gate leading to the barnyard.

Attempting to make out the figure, I moved to the back door, the upper half of which was solid glass. At that moment in my dream, Aaron came running toward the house, half stooped over, nervously glancing right and left. He was dressed in work fatigues. I quickly opened the door and waved him in. He grabbed me and jerked me to the floor, and we leaned our backs against the washer and dryer with our heads now below the line of vision from the wall-to-wall windows in front of us.

Fully aware in my dream that Aaron was currently deployed, I pleaded with him to tell me that he was okay. With a reassuring smile, he calmly explained he was being chased and just needed to hide out with me until he could catch his breath. I expressed how much I missed him and how worried I was. When I asked him what I could do to help, he said, "Mom, I just need you to pray for me. That's all."

After spending about ten minutes in the safety of our farmhouse, he told me it was time for him to head back out. I hugged him goodbye. He told me not to worry and then disappeared into the darkness.

I awoke suddenly and began praying for any form of protection I could think of for Aaron and his teammates.

A few days later, Aaron called home, and during that conversation, he told me about an incident which had happened *a few nights earlier.*

He and his teammates had just completed a successful raid on a Taliban stronghold. Of course, he wasn't able to elaborate, but I assumed they had snuck in and captured a high-value target. While fleeing the raid and heading back to base, they suddenly noticed vehicles fall in behind them in heated pursuit.

Aaron was driving the Humvee. He flipped the headlights off and began searching through night vision goggles for a place to pull off, take up position, and engage. The night was pitch black with almost zero visibility. With the engine wide open and dust clouds encircling the vehicle, Aaron suddenly felt the Humvee careening through the air—no traction beneath it.

He had driven off the side of a bridge.

Aaron's body was thrust forward as the Humvee made contact with earth, flipping then rolling down a steep embankment. He braced himself with planted feet, pressing his back hard against his seat—his chest and head tossing from side to side. His driver-side door shook loose of its latch and flung open. He somehow grabbed the door and pulled it to his side just before the vehicle flipped one more time, the hard ground now inches away.

Then finally, an abrupt halt.

Aaron explained that being able to pull that door shut saved his life.

He would have been ejected and most likely crushed beneath the weight of the vehicle had he not mustered the ability to grab that handle.

Everyone walked away uninjured.

Like my dear friend Sara carefully explained to me years earlier, God was always there—even when I couldn't be.

Aaron was a man who constantly defied the odds. He encountered *many* situations that should have cost him his life but didn't. His life was saturated with stories of escape or safety, both coming only from the hand of God.

One night in the desert of California, Aaron and his teammates participated in a training mission. They were practicing fast roping from a hovering chopper while fully outfitted for battle. (The SEAL gear adds at least sixty pounds to their already bulky frames.) Crosswinds and chopper blades stirred up the sand below and made an already black night even darker.

Aaron was third or fourth in line, and when his turn came, he grabbed the rope to begin his one-hundred-foot descent. No sooner had his feet left the chopper when he suddenly felt himself thrust upward then jerked free of the rope. A gust of wind had hit the chopper and momentarily tossed it about.

Aaron started free-falling toward the ground, slapping and snatching at the air trying to make contact with a rope he could no longer see. His buddies below began scrambling, trying to get themselves underneath him in hopes of breaking his fall.

Finally, Aaron felt that course thread of hope smack the palm of his hand. He grabbed on for dear life. While the rope slowed his descent, he never regained complete control. He crashed to the ground at a rapid rate of speed. Not knowing exactly what was going on, he felt himself flipping head over heel for what seemed like an eternity. He had landed on the edge of a steep hill, and momentum didn't allow any interruption of his fall. His teammates rushed over fully expecting to find him dead— or seriously injured—at the bottom of the hill. Instead, they were met by white teeth and huge eyes, climbing back up—completely uninjured. I can only imagine what left his mouth as he made his way toward his buddies—"Holy crap! Did you see that? That was awesome!"

✴

Because of incidents like the Humvee and the fast-roping, I had a unique confidence that not a hair on Aaron's head would be harmed without God's consent. In that confidence, I found tremendous peace.

Aaron never took God's hedge of protection for granted, either. In fact, he knew and understood the need for it more than most. If I had to choose one phrase to describe Aaron's strongest character trait, it would be this: He was never afraid to recognize or call out evil. Because our son gave his life to Christ at a very young age, he had a keen understanding of right and wrong, good and bad. Early on, we recognized that his most prominent spiritual gift was discernment. He used that gift well, and he used it boldly. He could see straight through any situation to the core of its merit or lack thereof, but more importantly, he had the fortitude to address it either way.

Aaron never rode the fence on an issue. He always knew exactly where he stood and was prepared to defend his position if necessary. It's not that he wouldn't listen to your side, but if you were wrong, he would call you on it. If you were right, he would side with you. His values were strong enough to withstand criticism because he was grounded in truth, and in his mind, truth was irrevocable. Period.

I believe that due to the nature of Aaron's character, he came under an extensive amount of spiritual warfare. In his youth, he was plagued by a recurring nightmare of a dark figure dressed like the queen of spades blocking his bedroom door, closing in on him until he woke in terror. We were stunned when in 2003 the military developed a set of playing cards to help troops identify the "most wanted" figures in Saddam Hussein's government. We all discussed how amazing it would be if one day Aaron killed the Queen of Spades or even ended up in a serious conflict with this character. (To my knowledge, that encounter never took place.)

Throughout Aaron's childhood, I had my own recurring nightmare as well. In my dream, I would walk into a church to find everyone staring at me, waiting for some type of reaction. Seeing a casket at the altar, I would walk forward, looking from side-to-side in an attempt to figure out my surroundings and the reason I was there in the first place. When I would finally reach the coffin, I would fall to my knees wailing at the sight. It was Aaron. As people would rush toward me, I would wake up, sobbing out loud.

This dream tortured me off and on for at least ten years. In retrospect, I believe God was showing me I would have the task of burying my own son and our lives and deaths would not follow the natural order. I also believe that in God's mercy, He used the nightmare to give me a unique sense of tenderness toward Aaron, which in turn, led to a life of few regrets.

★

In April 2010, Aaron started six months of the most rigorous evaluation in our nation's military, an all-consuming effort which, as expected, left almost no family time. After earning his highly-esteemed position at "the tip of the tip of the spear" in October 2010, Aaron told his father and me that the training required to enter the elite SEAL Team VI made BUD/S look like a cake walk. I didn't understand until the process was over just how demanding it was or how much Aaron had privately overcome to succeed.

To put this training in perspective, you need to understand that a SEAL has to have successfully completed at least two combat deployments before being considered for SEAL Team VI. The SEAL also must be noted—and recommended—as one of the best operators on his current team. Amazingly, out of that pool of those one-in-a-million candidates, only half actually succeed and complete the training for SEAL Team VI.

Aaron miraculously sailed through the evaluations even though—unbeknownst to his trainers—he had lost a great deal of the vision in his right eye. He had developed a form of macular degeneration and should have had experimental surgery months earlier, but he didn't want to put a cog in the wheel of his tremendous progress. The vision issues forced him to shoot from the opposite side of his body and also caused a near total lack of peripheral vision, which created much greater challenges when clearing a room.

My full understanding of just how amazing it was that Aaron had been able to compensate for his loss of eyesight didn't come until after Aaron had passed away and I read the book *FEARLESS: The Undaunted Courage and Ultimate Sacrifice of Navy SEAL Team SIX Operator Adam Brown*. In that book, I read about the unimaginable spirit of a man who overcame the loss of sight in his right eye, forcing him to retrain using his left eye. Never before had it dawned on me just how monumental of a task that was. Aaron had accomplished so much more than I had been aware of!

Adam Brown—a name etched in my soul. Adam lost his life on March 17, 2010, in the Hindu Kush Mountains of Afghanistan during a heated battle. Adam's death sent a shockwave through the Team VI community and personally affected my son's heart in a way that I'll never adequately convey. While Aaron had certainly seen his share of deaths through the years, something about Adam's death pierced him and caused him to take the loss personally. I'm sure, at least in part, this feeling was intensified because of the deep faith in Christ that marked Adam's character and life—something Aaron absolutely identified with. Adam was not only a brother in arms but also a brother in Christ.

After Adam's death, a short film was made and published online in his honor. Aaron requested that I watch the film, and he refused to rest until I did. I started it several times but had to turn it off. The story was so well done that Adam's personality leaped off the screen straight into my heart. It was too much…too painful…too real. My heart ached with each attempt, but Aaron kept insisting. Day after day he would call and ask "have you watched it yet?"

I explained to him how difficult it was for me to sit through the film knowing that one day it could be my son…my loss.

Aaron never let up.

"You need to watch all of it, Mom. You need to know this man and his sacrifice."

On the next phone call, he asked again. "Have you watched it yet? Mom, every American needs to watch this. They need to know that men like Adam Brown lived…and died…for them."

I finally watched the entire film and then encouraged others to do the same.

But that film wrecked me.

Little did I know that less than a year later Aaron would be working with not only the same SEAL *team* Adam was fighting with when he lost his life, but also the same exact *squad* and *troop*.

Chapter Sixteen

God Is Good

GOD IS GOOD. HE KNOWS what lies ahead and often pours His love out in advance, knowing what we'll need to make it through what's waiting down the road.

During the ten months before Aaron's death, we spent more time together as a family than in any other year since he had joined the military. In addition, he had been able to visit all his loved ones back in Northwest Tennessee on multiple occasions—something which had never happened before. He created a social media page and spent that year reconnecting with many friends from his youth, including Caleb Chandler, the one he had lit that bottle rocket with all those years before.

Aaron took a weekend trip to Nashville where he spent time with another one of his high school buddies, Will David Coleman. I guess they had a pretty good time because during the next conversation I had with Aaron he told me he wanted to move to Nashville when he left the Teams. He had visited the Music City many times in his youth with his father and me, but I guess visiting as an adult was an entirely different experience. He had seen the world by now but insisted Nashville was by far the coolest place he had ever been.

In late October 2010, I turned the corner leading to my house and was shocked to see Aaron's truck in our driveway. He, Kimberly, and Reagan were already inside, waiting for Billy and me to arrive home.

Since Billy's and my thirtieth wedding anniversary was only a few days away, I assumed our kids had planned something special. I didn't care what that special something was—it was just an incredible blessing to have all of them home and the whole family together. Later that evening, my mom showed up, all the way from Tennessee. After the hugs and excitement had died down, I looked at the kids and asked what was going on.

"Well, we all got together and bought you guys a photo shoot on the beach for your anniversary," Tara answered. "We knew how much it would mean to you if the whole family could be in the pictures."

I was stunned and so incredibly happy. I remember thinking to myself that night, as I dropped into bed beside Billy—completely exhausted from all the laughter we had shared throughout the evening—*we really do have it all, don't we?*

I felt like the luckiest woman in the world.

We spent the next day enjoying one another's company and making memories.

Tara and her husband Adam's oldest daughter, Annabelle, adored Aaron. She always had. She clung to him like white on rice, hanging on his every move. The deep affection and attention were absolutely reciprocated. On the contrary, their youngest, Lyla, was terrified of Aaron. Her reaction always gave us a good chuckle. All Aaron had to do was look at her and she would well up with tears and reach for her mother. Naturally, Aaron thought it was hilarious to scare little Lyla. He would sneak up behind her highchair, place his face right beside hers, and wait for her to notice him. As soon as she saw him, she would lunge her body to the other side of the chair and, of course, Aaron was on *that* side waiting for her. The result brought the whole table to a roar. (Our family has always had a lot of fun scaring each other, so Aaron got that trait honestly. Oh, the stories I could tell!)

Aaron gave little one-year-old Reagan a pretty good scare as well that day. Reagan was laying on his belly fussing. Aaron threw on a were-wolf mask, crawled up behind him, and flipped him over. The poor little guy nearly came off the floor in a startled jolt, letting out an ear-piercing shriek. Aaron pulled the mask off, snatched Reagan up, and literally writhed with laughter. Seeing that I caught the whole thing on video, Aaron flipped around and wheezed out, "Don't put that on Facebook!" I made no promises.

Later that afternoon, when we arrived at the beach for our photo shoot, we were met by not only Billy's parents (who had also come in from Tennessee) but our Pastor and a whole host of our closest friends.

Unbeknownst to us, our kids had spent months planning the photo shoot plus a sunset vow renewal on our favorite beach, The House of Refuge.

The ceremony was breathtaking.

With my husband—the love of my youth—before me, the Atlantic Ocean to my left, and our loved ones to the right, we recited once again the promises we had made thirty years earlier—the promises we had never broken. I never felt more loved...or thankful.

The evening wasn't over. Tara, Ana, and Aaron had created a full-fledged wedding reception at the home of our friends, Hoss and Linda Wiggins. We arrived to soft music flowing over beautifully appointed tables—flowers and candles in the center of each, an over-the-top spread of delicious hors d'oeuvres, and a lavish buffet. They had even set up a head table—adorned with china and stemware—so Billy and I could face our guests. The entire night was magical.

As her gift to us, Tara had made a photo book that included snap-shots and letters from everyone in our family. When we turned to my father's page, there was a letter from him, written by Tara. We were amazed at how much her words sounded like dad's. (He had been gone for nine years.) Our hearts ached as together we all longed for his presence. I couldn't stop crying enough to finish reading the letter out loud,

Our entire family on The House of Refuge beach at sunset

Cracking up over Aaron's comment about having to follow Tara's "Daddy Frank" page. From left to right, it's me, Billy, Aaron, Kimberly, Tara, and Ana.

so Tara took the book and shared the final words. By the end, we were all in tears at the many memories that flooded our minds, and we could barely bring ourselves to continue.

When we finally turned the page, we found Aaron's note—all three sentences of it. After reading the only three sentences on the page, Billy chuckled and said, "Wow, Son, you really outdid yourself, huh?"

"Okay, that's not fair!" Aaron blurted out with complete exasperation. "Tara didn't tell me she was gonna be channeling our dead grandfather! How come I have to go right after Daddy Frank? How am I supposed to compete with that?"

The entire room erupted with laughter.

Our sweet friend and photographer Casi Brush flawlessly captured every emotion of that incredible evening. She later gifted Billy and me with a framed photo of our entire family, captioned "All Because Two People Fell In Love."

★

Next came Christmas. Aaron and Kimberly decided to spend almost two weeks with us in Florida for the holidays. Man, did we ever have fun!

Billy and I had purchased BB guns for each of the grandchildren knowing full well none of them were really old enough to use the guns. But, we thought it would be fun anyway. We bought pink for the girls and the classic Red Ryder for Reagan.

As soon as all the gifts were opened on Christmas morning, Aaron grabbed Reagan's gun, shrugged a shoulder toward Adam while opening the back door, and said, "Hey, Adam, grab one of those pink ones over there! Let's go!" Again…laughter.

During that visit, Billy and Aaron tried nearly every day to take the boat out for some deep-sea fishing. However, in the winter, the ocean is rough. They woke up on the very last morning of vacation and knew it was a now or never thing. Billy's friend Sal came over to help get the boat ready. Both Aaron and Billy wanted to take Reagan along on the trip, but after some deliberation and knowing it was going to be a long, rough day, they finally looked at each other and agreed to take him next time.

Oh, the plans we make thinking life will always follow the paths created by our own minds.

Christmas 2010—One of my last photos with my boy

Chapter Seventeen

I'll See You in November

O N June 3, 2011, Aaron and Kimberly welcomed their second child into the world—Catherine Chamberlyn Vaughn. When Aaron called moments after the birth to tell me it was a little girl, I began praying that he would consider winding down his dangerous career. Since men are generally much more protective—by nature—over their daughters than their sons, I was hopeful.

After Chamberlyn's birth, Aaron and Kimberly relocated to Kimberly's parents' home in Northern Virginia since Aaron's upcoming deployment would leave her with no help otherwise. Reagan was twenty-one months old at the time.

Two weeks later, Tara and I, along with her two little girls, jumped in the car, buckled up, and made the long haul from Florida to Washington, D.C. Ana stayed behind, unable to get time off from her job. Billy, who had been out of state for work, met us there on our second day. Together as a family, we celebrated the birth of our newest addition and had an early celebration of Aaron's thirtieth birthday, which was only days away.

Watching my son hold his baby girl was an incredible experience. He kept saying over and over again, "Isn't she so beautiful? I've never seen anything so beautiful." He was mesmerized.

Holding his beautiful baby girl.
He only had three weeks with her before he left
on his next deployment to Afghanistan.

The typical Vaughn family fun that occurs whenever we are all together was a little difficult to embrace because Aaron's deployment to Afghanistan was rapidly approaching. Even though it was hard and our time together that weekend was short, our days were filled with incredible memories. In any other situation those memories probably wouldn't seem significant, but in light of what lay ahead for us, their significance is now immeasurable.

Our family, in large part, is very musically inclined. At that time, Tara and I were both singing for private events and leading worship in our local church. Aaron had been learning to play the guitar and had brought it home with him on his last few visits. And although I had known since his childhood that Aaron was also gifted vocally, I had no idea how good he had actually become until he called me downstairs on the first morning of our visit. Timidly, he asked me to listen to a rough recording he had made on his iPhone of just him singing and playing his guitar.

I listened in stunned silence to the Aaron Vaughn versions of "The Ride" by Hank Williams, Jr., and "Simple Man" by Lynyrd Skynyrd. Aaron's voice blew me away. As soon as the second song ended, I called Tara down to listen as well. She was equally moved by the level of talent that we previously had no idea existed. Knowing that Aaron already loved Nashville, Tara suggested he go ahead and move there when he retired from the Teams so he could try his hand as a country music artist.

We sat downstairs in Kimberly's parents' basement for hours, Aaron playing guitar and all three of us singing together while Reagan crawled up and down the basement steps, giggling and smiling. Since our playlists weren't the same, we struggled to find songs we all knew, but we had trouble pulling up chord tabs because of a weak Internet connection. We ended up just muddling through as best we could, enjoying each other's company and our newfound commonality.

Nearing the end of that unforgettable time in the basement, Tara asked Aaron if he knew a certain song.

"Oh, yeah! I love that song, but I don't know the chords."

They attempted to struggle through it but finally gave up and made a pact that before the next time they got together that they would both learn "If I Die Young" by The Band Perry.

Then, we all left the basement and headed to a nearby restaurant for lunch. After an hour or so at the restaurant, Chamberlyn started fussing, wanting to be fed and put down for a nap. I offered to take Kimberly and all the kids home while Aaron and Tara finished their lunch and conversation. This was a God-ordained moment in time meant just for my daughter and my son—their last "alone time" on this side of eternity.

As the two of them sat together by themselves for the first time in many years, they rehearsed childhood stories, laughed together, spoke of their current lives and future dreams, and remembered just how much they missed that kind of togetherness.

Tara took the time to tell Aaron how proud she was of him, how much she honored and appreciated all he had become, and how deeply she loved him. Money cannot buy moments like that. Little did she know these would be some of her last words to the hero and best friend of her childhood. After the next day, she would never see his face again.

That next day went by in a blur: breakfast at iHop, the NEX (Navy Exchange) for supplies, lunch and ice cream, loads of snuggle time with the grandbabies, and then dinner somewhere. I don't recall where.

What I do recall is what happened next.

We all returned to the hotel where Billy, Tara, and I were staying. We wanted to spend just a little more time together before our departure early the following morning. My memory captured every detail of the room…the corner chair where Kimberly held the baby, the window overlooking all of our vehicles, and the two queen-sized beds Billy and I shared with Tara and our granddaughters. About an hour after arriving at the hotel, Kimberly decided to take Reagan and Chamberlyn home. It had been a long day for all of them, and sadly, nighttime had come.

Not long after Kimberly left, everyone fell asleep…except for Aaron and me.

The time had once again come for one of our incredibly special, consecrated through decades of repetition, late-night talks. Like always, it started around ten and ended around three the next morning. While these talks were typically sprinkled with jokes and laughter, none of that occurred that night.

Our conversation was serious and made up of questions like "You'll be a lot safer on this deployment than any of the others you've been on, right? Since you'll be with SEAL Team VI, right?"

"Actually, this will be the most dangerous deployment I've ever been on, Mom. We're gonna be working in a really bad area."

Something in my head refused to hear Aaron's response. I kept making light of the serious nature of his comments. I swept to the back of my mind every warning he gave me that something would be very different about this deployment. Maybe it was because there was absolutely *no* fear in his voice, but instead, he was resolute and anxious to deploy. It's odd that my brain didn't process what was happening because never in the past had Aaron and I had a conversation where such statements were made.

"Mom, this team has done missions where everyone was advised to write letters to their loved ones…just in case. Suicide missions where they felt like there'd be a good chance they'd never come home."

And somehow still—I missed it.

I was laser-focused on November and the huge family reunion we were planning back in Tennessee, the home of Aaron's youth and the home of nearly all of our living relatives. And, this was a short deployment.

Four little months.

It would be over before we knew it, and we would all be together at Granny and Papa's house (Billy's parents), nestled on the warm, familiar farm where our family began.

It was going to be awesome with lots of laughter and lots of little kids from our newest generation running wildly through the house. We would most definitely blow something up since explosives of some sort always went off when all the Vaughn boys got together. We would take family pictures and have barbecues. We would shoot at targets in the ravine off the back porch, and Granny's deck would be covered with shell casings trapped in the crevices between the wood planks, making them impossible to sweep up.

Aaron and the rest of the men would go hunting, a Vaughn holiday tradition he had been a part of since childhood. We would all gather around Uncle Jerry's, Adam's, Larry's and Aaron's guitars and sing until our throats were raw. My mom would come over from Knoxville and spend at least a few of those days with us. Aaron would box in the backyard with his younger cousins, Trey and Ethan. Some of his teammates from West Memphis or friends from Nashville might even come up and spend a day...

I had plans. Big plans.

That's all I could focus on that night. Maybe it was a matter of self-preservation, or maybe just complete naïveté that anything bad could happen to *my* son. It had always been *someone else's* son before. Whatever the case, it never crossed my mind that this could—would—be our last night together.

Finally, the dreaded words spilled out of Aaron's mouth. "Well, I'd better go so you can get some sleep. You've got a long drive ahead of you tomorrow."

Our visit was over. Aaron woke his sister and her daughters to hug them goodbye. Though they exchanged "I love yous," their eyes never really opened. Billy woke up and composed himself, and then the three of us walked downstairs.

Just the three of us.

As it was in the beginning, it was in our final moments: me…Billy… and our boy.

The glass hotel doors slid apart and the warm summer breeze, moist with morning dew, blew quietly across our skin. With nothing left to say but goodbye, I hugged my son for the final time while Billy stood by, waiting to walk Aaron to his truck. I expected the same hug I had been receiving for years. Since Aaron was 6'4", our hugs were awkward. I would lay my head on the side of his chest and wrap my arms around his waist while he would wrap one arm around me and pat my back with the other hand.

But this time was different.

Aaron grabbed me with both arms, pulled me close, laid his cheek on top of my head, and squeezed me like he hadn't done since childhood. He held onto me for an unusually long time—so long that I actually tried to pull away after a few seconds. But Aaron tightened his grip. I just stood there holding onto him until he decided to let go.

That shook me.

Backing away, but now gripping both of his arms in my hands, I looked up and asked, "Is everything okay, Son?"

"It's fine, Mom. Just go on inside. I'll call you tomorrow."

"Are you sure?"

"I'm sure." A sweet but hesitant smile slowly spread on his beautiful face.

As I released my grip and stepped backward toward the door, I glanced at Billy, wondering if he noticed what had just taken place. He hadn't. He was looking down, scuffing the concrete sidewalk with the ball of his shoe, and dreading his final goodbye.

"Go on in, Mom. You need sleep." Both hands now in his jean pockets, Aaron gestured toward the door with his head and right shoulder.

As I turned to walk inside after we exchanged our final "I love you," I could sense that Aaron hadn't moved. Just as I entered the sliding glass doors, I glanced over my shoulder and saw that, sure enough, he hadn't budged. Aaron just stood there staring at me. In retrospect, it was as if he knew in his heart this would be the last time he would ever see his mom.

Puzzled, I spun around demanding again, "Son, are you okay?"

"I'm fine, Mom. You need to go on in and get some sleep."

Billy looked up and gave me a nod in the direction of the door. Worry flooded my heart, and for the first time that night, I felt fear. But being a pro at choking down those fears through years of watching my boy leave on deployment after deployment, I regained my composure.

"I'll see you in November, Son. I love you so much. I'm so proud of you."

"I love you too, Mom."

As I entered the lobby, I turned one last time. Aaron and his dad were finally making their way to the truck. And that was it—my last vision of my boy here on earth, walking side-by-side with his dad.

We briefly spoke the following day during my drive back to South Florida and then again for the final time a few days later as Aaron was boarding the plane. He always called us just before taking off for an overseas deployment. After a hurried rehearsal of our plans for Thanksgiving and a quick exchange of our final goodbyes, I spoke words that had been shared between us many times in the past.

"You bring yourself home to me, you hear?"

But instead of the usual, "I will, Mom," his response stopped me in my tracks. With all the tenderness and humility one could muster, he said, "I hate it when people say that to me."

Taken aback, I fumbled for a recovery, while doing my best to keep the conversation light. "Then go kick some butt!"

With a chuckle in his voice, he said, "That's better. I can do that."

And once again, I carelessly threw aside any notion that those words could have been some type of forewarning. They never crossed my mind again.

Until August 6.

Chapter Eighteen

August Sixth

(Portions of the next few chapters were written by Aaron's father Billy and first appeared in "Betrayed: The Shocking True Story of Extortion 17")

Billy

AUGUST 6, 2011, FELL ON a Saturday. Early that morning around three o'clock, I woke up in Burlington, Washington (north of Seattle). I started my day with a prayer and asked the Lord's protection over my family. At the end of my prayer, I repeated that request and I remember saying "especially for Aaron, whatever he is doing today."

That day, my family was spread out across the globe. Aaron was on deployment in Afghanistan. His wife Kimberly was in Virginia with her parents. My wife was at home in Florida, as were my daughters, my son-in-law, and my other grandchildren. I was on the opposite corner of the country on my way to deliver a camper trailer to Vancouver Island, British Columbia.

It was a pitch-black morning, hours before the sunrise. I was on the West Coast surrounded by nothing but land on Interstate 5. As I always did while on the road in the mornings, I tuned in to Fox News on satellite radio. But on *this* morning, I caught a quick report that "thirty-one" (the number would later be revised to thirty) American soldiers had been killed when their chopper crashed after being shot down in Afghanistan.

My heart stopped for a second.

I said silently, "Lord, I pray that Aaron wasn't on that chopper."

But, just as that thought entered my mind, I felt ashamed. What right did I have to even think such a thing? Thirty-one other families had lost someone they loved. Of course, I never wanted Aaron hurt, but I realized that if *my* son was not involved in the shoot down, someone else's son was.

Moments later, the story came across the radio with additional details. This time, the report was more specific. The reporter used the words "Special Forces."

Finally, a third report came. I heard the words "Special Forces with Afghan Commandos in the Wardak Province," and it hit far too close to home. Each update painted a more vivid picture. Special Forces. Wardak Province. Working with Afghan Commandos. No survivors.

During that last weekend before his deployment, Aaron had explained to me that he would be working in Wardak Province. I also knew that Navy SEALs always took Afghan Commandos and interpreters with them on their nighttime raids.

It had to be Aaron's team…

✫

Karen

At 4:45 A.M. on August 6, my head popped up off my pillow. In those days I was a very heavy sleeper, so I felt startled. I instinctively grabbed the navy blue rubber wristband I wore each time Aaron was deployed. On the band, in bright gold letters were two simple words— Navy SEALs. I wore this band to remind myself to pray for Aaron and for his teammates. As I sat up holding the band, I wasn't afraid. I didn't feel any sense of dread. I just felt a need to pray.

So, that's what I did.

Our youngest daughter, Ana, was spending the night with a friend, and since Billy was out of town on business, I was completely alone. Unable to fall back asleep, I decided to get up. I was frustrated since this was Saturday—the only day of the week I got to sleep in—but I tried to relax knowing I would be able to nap later in the day if needed. I straightened up the house, watched a little bit of television, and then around 6:30, I went back to bed.

One hour later the phone startled me awake. Frustrated, I answered with a gruff "Hello."

On the other end of the line I heard a voice, trembling, speak words I'll never forget.

"Karen, I have something to tell you, but I don't want to." Billy's tone jerked my weary body to full attention, my mind racing, wondering what could be so important that he would call at 4:30 a.m. his time. And why did he sound so frightened?

"What's wrong, honey?"

"Karen…" Billy didn't say anything more.

"Honey, what is it? Tell me? What's wrong?"

"Karen…I don't want you to be afraid…and I've really tried hard not to call, but I had to. A helicopter was shot down in Afghanistan last night and thirty Americans are dead. And hon…Aaron could be involved." He rushed to add, "I'm not saying he is. I'm just saying we need to see if we can reach him."

My mind staggered into a level of confusion and fear I had never known before. I knew instantly it was very serious if *Billy* was this concerned. We had heard of crashed choppers before. We had watched the news with a distant sense of dread through dozens, if not hundreds, of reports of fallen soldiers over the previous nine years. Billy had never called me in fear. Something was terribly wrong.

We both knew it.

We both felt it.

I recalled how I had been startled awake only hours earlier. What was happening? My mind suddenly was unable to function. Fear swept over me like a raging volcano, my flesh screaming for relief—for a sign that my boy was okay.

With my voice barely unable to escape my lips, I whispered, "What can I do, Billy? What do you want me to do?"

Full panic set in as he began explaining what he knew and what he thought our next course of action should be. "What I think you should do is try to reach some of his buddies to see if they know anything. Try that first and call me back. Can you do that? Are you okay?"

"Okay, let me think. Let me think. Okay, I'll call you right back."

I tried calling Brad Cavner, Aaron's best friend and fellow SEAL. Brad lived in San Diego, so it didn't surprise me when he didn't answer at 4:40 A.M. PST.

Next, I decided to call Ana. By this time, she had left her friend's house to go to work. I told her what I knew and tried to assure her that I didn't believe Aaron was involved, and then I asked her to continue trying to reach Brad for me. Ana was very

Attempting to reach Brad via Facebook

Karen R. Vaughn ▸ Brad Cavner
August 6, 2011 · 👥

Brad - please call me ▉▉▉▉▉

👍 Like　　💬 Comment

close to Brad, and he had taken her under his wing like she was his own little sister. They talked frequently so it wasn't unusual for her to try and call him.

I quickly realized that all of the team guys I had contact numbers for were from the West Coast. Knowing I wouldn't be able to reach any of them, I turned to Facebook. I got online to see if there was any chatter, any clues. Nothing.

I texted the wife of the only team guy I knew on the East Coast to ask if she had heard from her husband. *Is James OK?* I asked. (In my state of confusion, I called her husband by the wrong name...the name of another one of their friends.)

Immediately, she wrote back *Is James not home???* (I later realized she was attempting to verify if she should be looking for *his* name as well on the long list of deceased friends trickling in hour after heart-wrenching hour.)

I mean Joe, sorry!

He's fine. Have you heard from Aaron?

I haven't. Please let me know if you hear from anyone. Thank God Joe is OK! Thank God!

I will. Don't worry, Karen.

I called Billy back to tell him I had been unable to gather any information. We discussed calling Kimberly to see if she had been in contact with Aaron, but quickly agreed we didn't want to put her through what we were experiencing until we knew more. She was only nine weeks out of childbirth. We wanted to protect her as long as possible, praying there would be resolution at any second.

Billy asked if I knew the number for her parents' landline. Maybe we could get information from them without alerting Kimberly. What a great idea...such clear thinking.

I called and reached her mother. I asked if Kimberly was awake and if they were aware of what was going on. The answer was no on both accounts. After filling her in, we decided together it was best not to wake her. I promised to stay in touch with any new information.

With desperation clawing at my throat, making it difficult to breathe, I called Billy back to give him an update, and then made two additional calls. These calls weren't for answers—they were for help. I was breaking down.

The first was to my newfound friend Angie, a prayer warrior who I knew would fall to her face before God on Aaron's behalf.

As soon as Angie answered, the words burst out, "I think my son is dead! Please, please, oh, God, please pray." I remember how tight my throat felt as those unfathomable words spewed out.

The second call was to my sister-in-law, Kelly, back on our farm in Tennessee. The farm where our slithering SEAL-in-training had spent his childhood years playing, growing, laughing, and learning.

Again, but this time with more control, "Kelly, a chopper was shot down in Afghanistan. Everyone onboard is dead. I'm afraid Aaron might be gone. Please...pray."

That's all I remember.

By this time, Tara and her two baby girls arrived at my house. Billy had called her to explain what he knew at that point and told her she should come be with me…just in case. I could see in her eyes the steady resolve she had learned from her father. She walked in bearing a Cappuccino Blast and a bag full of donuts. She spoke hope, and hope, alone. Having her and her little girls there brought the first sense of calm I had felt since the abrupt phone call that shook me from sleep.

We discussed that it was likely we hadn't heard from Aaron yet because he would surely be too busy right now to make a call home.

"Can you imagine the chaos going on over there after such a massive loss of life?" Tara said.

I agreed but still insisted he would have made some attempt to reach me—or Kimberly—since he had to know how terrified all of us would be while waiting to hear he was not involved.

I sat down at my computer again and saw that word of the shoot down had reached Facebook. In fact, my cousin Darla had shared the breaking news story that a chopper had been shot down during the night, killing thirty Americans. She accompanied the post with a comment of her own: *Please pray for these families.*

My comment was first: *Darla, this could be OUR family. Please pray for Aaron.*

Her immediate response: *HE'S NOT HOME?????*

I didn't reply.

I called Billy and we decided together that it was time to call Kimberly and get her involved.

I dialed the phone and this time Kimberly's father answered. Before I could finish my first sentence, he interrupted me.

"Karen, it's not good."

"Oh, I know!" I replied, thinking he was talking about how much the details indicated possible involvement of Aaron's team.

"Karen, listen to me." His voice was quivering and breathy. "Aaron was on the helicopter." There was a long pause. I could hear his shaking breath and could sense that he was searching for some way to deliver this unthinkable news. Finally, it came. "And there were no survivors."

The world stopped spinning.

No words can adequately describe a moment like that.

The confusion. The disbelief. The struggle your brain undergoes trying to comprehend the magnitude of what you've just heard.

"No, no, no, no, NO!" I screamed as I fell backward into the chair I had been sitting in minutes before.

"What is it, Mom?" Tara pleaded, although she already knew after watching all color drain from my skin. My precious daughter, choking back the pain ripping at her soul, took control. "Mom, give me the phone."

Only then did I realize Kimberly's father was still on the line. Tara took the phone from my shaking hands and calmly gathered the information I was unable to ask for.

He explained that U.S. Navy officers were at the door as we spoke. Kimberly had collapsed to the ground—her mother grabbing the baby before she hit the floor.

And Aaron was…dead.

I thought for just a moment he would tell Tara something contrary to what he had told me. Maybe something like "they're still searching for survivors" or "actually, they've only told us they 'think' he was on the chopper."

When Tara hung up the phone, I asked, "What did he say?"

"You're going to be all right, Mom." I don't remember anything else she told me.

I felt the life leaving my body.

Suddenly, I stood up in an attempt to snap myself into action. My legs, as though unattached from my brain, began running through the house, for lack of any better options. My daughter, following behind me, kept grabbing my arm and coaxing me to lay down so I wouldn't pass out. But laying down was something I could not do. I felt like I had turned into stone. My ears roared, and darkness flooded my eyes each time I blinked.

I remember thinking the whole time that this is exactly how people react on television and how I never thought those reactions were sincere. Now, I was learning this really *is* what you do. At the same time, I was scolding myself for being so dramatic and kept thinking about how *strange* it was, at a time like this, to be picturing movies I had seen. I felt like I was standing above myself screaming, *"Pull it together!"*

I finally landed on my bed. A volatile reaction overtook my inmost parts, as if everything inside of me intended to implode. I pushed past the physical pain and began trying to process names of people I needed to call. I wondered how on earth I could speak the very words my body was revolting against.

Tara, maintaining an unimaginable calm, kept saying, "You don't need to call anyone yet, Mom. Please just be still for a minute. I'll take care of calling everyone."

We sat staring at each other in bewildered silence until finally Tara spoke again, "Do you want me to call Dad?"

My mind went numb—*Dad! Oh my Lord. Aaron is dead, and Billy doesn't know!*

Paralyzed now, nearly unable to formulate a sound, I nodded that she should make the call.

★

Billy

While standing on the loading ramp for the ferry to Vancouver Island, some 3,500 miles from home, I engaged in a brief conversation with two Canadian fishermen, but my mind and heart were on an event that had occurred some 7,000 miles away. Then our discussion was interrupted by a call from my daughter.

What I heard through Tara's sobs were three words which I never could have prepared myself to hear:

"Daddy, he's dead."

Tara, married with a family of her own, had not called me "Daddy" in years. There was no script for this kind of thing, no preparation, only guttural reaction.

Her words cut to the depths of my heart. I didn't have a response, just "Okay, baby, I'll call you right back."

That call had come way too quickly. With those words, it was final.

Hope for my son's life was lost.

As soon as I hung up the phone with my daughter, I climbed into my truck to drive it up the loading ramp. Almost instantly, my sister Kelly called.

"Are you alright?"

"Yeah, I'm alright," I said, while managing the steering wheel to load the truck on the ferry.

"Are you sure?" Kelly's voice was full of doubt.

"What do you know?" I asked.

"Well, Karen called and asked us to pray that Aaron wouldn't be on the chopper."

"Aaron was on the chopper." The words felt surreal. "He's gone, Kelly."

"Oh no, Billy! Oh no!" I had never heard my sister cry with such desperation before.

Kelly agreed to drive to our parents' home to be with them after I called with the news. I called them just as they were getting out of bed. My dad answered from the living room, and I immediately said, "There's been a helicopter shot down in Afghanistan."

"They are talking about it right now on the TV."

At that moment, my mom picked up the phone in their bedroom. I could still hear the television in the background. My dad was watching Fox News. I thought my father had handed over the phone to my mom, and I assumed I was just talking to her when I said, "Aaron is gone."

Mom fell over on their bed from the shock. Dad was still on the line in the living room, and I heard him cry out, "Oh no, no!"

When my mom managed to speak again, she asked, "Oh no, what happened?"

"A helicopter was shot down, and he was in it."

"Oh Son, where are you?"

"I'm on a ferry," I replied.

"Does Karen know? Who's with her?"

"Tara." I said. "Mom, I prayed for him this morning, and he was already gone."

My mind flooded with chaos and confusion.

Then my mom with her soft, reassuring voice said, "Son, I'm so sorry you are so far away and I can't comfort you, and I'm so sorry that Karen is in Florida. All we can do right now is stand on our faith because that's all we have."

We ended our conversation, and by this time, my Dodge and the trailer were parked. It had been a dark morning.

Just as I set foot on the deck, a glow of light began to flood the sky as the sun rose. After all the phone calls and engine noise, now all I could hear were the waves embracing the ship's hull as I slowly made my way to Vancouver Island. I stood on the top deck of the ferry, facing northwest, looking out at the Strait of Georgia between Vancouver Island and the mainland. The light intensified as it reflected on the ocean's surface, and in all of my deliberately suppressed emotions, I was now overwhelmed by the stunning image of nature confronting me. I watched the incredible sunrise, the red of dawn, and felt as though it was just God, Aaron, and me.

Finally, I said, "It's a beautiful morning, isn't it, Son?"

Chapter Nineteen

But God Was There

Karen

After Tara had hung up from talking to her dad, she began making other calls. Her first call was to Ana. With tears streaming down her face, voice shaking, she said, "Ana, you need to come home right away."

Already knowing the answer, Ana asked, "Why?" I suppose she was praying for a different response.

"Because he's dead."

That's all Tara could bring herself to say.

Tara then called her husband, Adam. She called our pastor, and finally, our closest friends.

Somehow God gave me the strength to call my brother, Kurt, and then my mother. I chose to call my brother first so I could ask him to send someone to Mom's house so she wouldn't be alone after hearing the news. (Neither of us lived in her hometown.)

I'll never forget the calmness I found when I made that call to my brother. It would be the first time my lips formed those unspeakable words: "Kurt, Aaron's been killed. I need you to call someone and get them to Mom's house. I'm calling her next."

Aaron's been killed. The words tasted like bile, revolting against all of my senses.

Then I called my mother.

"Mom, I need you to sit down. Tell me when you're sitting."

"Okay? What's going on?"

"Just tell me when you're sitting, okay?" I was certain this news could send her to the floor.

"What is it, honey?" I know she sensed the seriousness of my tone.

"Are you sitting?"

"Yes."

"Mom, I don't know how to tell you this, but Aaron was killed last night. He's gone, Mom."

As her heart-wrenching cries of anguish began, my steady resolve disappeared. I had to get off the phone. I don't recall what else was said, but I stayed strong until support for her had arrived and the call ended. Knowing how deeply and passionately I loved my own grandchildren, I kept thinking that I could not imagine what she was feeling and how her heart must be breaking.

I remember sitting on the end of my bed, staring into my dressing mirror at a shell of the person who had crawled from beneath those sheets only an hour earlier. I just kept thinking there had to be a mistake. Surely, *someone* had survived the crash. How could they *all* be dead? Someone *had* to call and tell us they had found Aaron alive. They only *thought* he had been on the chopper.

Finally, I mustered the strength to call Billy again and then Kimberly. Billy let me know that he had called his own parents and had spoken with Kelly. All I remember saying to him was "I'm so sorry. I'm so, so sorry. Oh God, I'm so sorry, honey. You've lost your son!" What else was there to say? Those were similar to the only words I could muster in my conversation with Kimberly as well.

I realized how hard life was going to be for each of us without Aaron. I knew, without a shadow of a doubt, there had never been a father who loved and cherished his boy more than Billy loved and cherished Aaron. I knew Kimberly had waited so faithfully to find the love of her life and now, three short years after her marriage, she was widowed with a baby and a toddler.

None of it seemed fair. None of it seemed acceptable.

As my mind grasped for clarity and direction, extraordinary truths penetrated my thoughts. I realized we were each going to be dealing with a very unique loss. A father-son relationship is nothing like that of a mother and her son. Nor does a parent-child or sibling relationship have anything in common with the bond of marriage. Death is personal, and no one should ever tell you "I know how you feel." I couldn't have made that statement to my own husband even though we had both just lost our only son.

I remember speaking out loud, over and over again, that morning, "We do not grieve as those who have no hope." I realized, within seconds of learning that Aaron was, in fact, gone, that heavy decisions lay before me…life-altering decisions. I understood with great clarity that I needed to press toward what I knew, not what I felt. If I succumbed to my feelings, I would never make it.

Oh, how many times over the years did I give my children the same advice God was now whispering to my soul: "Take every thought captive, Karen…and make those thoughts obedient to what you know about Me. Only then will you be able to demolish every argument or pretense that sets itself up against your knowledge of Who I Am and what my desires are for you." (paraphrase of II Corinthians 10:5)

Life and death hung in the balance.

Literally.

I had never felt such an overwhelming desire to go "home." Not because I didn't love and cherish the things still in my presence, but because I could not imagine surviving for a day, much less the rest of my natural life, under the weight of grief I was experiencing physically. It would have been impossible, but God was there. Though I could feel nothing else, I could feel Him. He was holding me, loving me, promising me that He had not forsaken me.

Something in my brain began to function…to fight. The "mom" in me kicked in, just the way God had designed me. I began to consider all the collateral damage that could come from this one moment in time if I didn't respond in faith. I could see the battlefield before me. I had remarkable clarity that, if I quit, others may quit as well. I also knew that even if others didn't quit alongside me, I would forever change the nature of our family if *I* did. If I nurtured my grief, I would destroy everyone, the very ones who were going to need me now more than ever.

I kept telling myself that "they'll never make it if they lose you, too, Karen."

These thoughts pushed me forward.

✸

I was astounded at how quickly word spread that morning. I had barely finished my call with my mother when friends began arriving. With each new face at my door, a new level of reality sank in. I had always been on the *other side* of that door in the past. It was completely surreal being the one *inside*.

Ana finally made it home, and I remember thinking to myself, *Oh, God, I have nothing to offer her.* She was only eighteen, and her big brother was dead. She looked so helpless, so confused, so lost, so small. In the flurry of friends, she retreated to her bedroom, and I don't recall seeing much more of her that day. I grieved more deeply knowing that I had no comfort to give her when she needed me so desperately.

In that moment, I was empty. I wasn't sure anyone or anything would ever be okay again.

✸

Many phone calls from distant friends came in that morning, but none offered quite as much comfort as the one from my long-time spiritual mother and confidant, Sara Williams. Sara was the one who had patiently instructed me all those years before that my children were not my own and that they belonged to God. And now, with both of us stricken by the full scope of this level of faith, she began to pray over me.

Not *for* me—over me.

I had never experienced such peace in the midst of such earth-shattering despair. All around me nothing but chaos and confusion reigned. But in that earpiece, as the promises of God were being rehearsed to my battered heart, I heard calm assurance that God had not forsaken me—or Aaron.

During her prayer, she spoke something close to the following: "And God, we know in those last few seconds of Aaron's life, *You* were there. God, I can picture a host of angels surrounding that helicopter, perhaps even Jesus, Himself...waiting for Aaron. Waiting for that glorious moment when he would finally come home. And Lord, we know you swept Aaron up into Your beautiful, strong arms before that helicopter ever made contact with the ground. He breathed his last breath in your arms, Jesus...safely home."

Praise God. Praise God. I envisioned it as she spoke.

Aaron's time here was but a vapor. Oh, if we could all recognize the same about ourselves. If we could only grasp the fact that we're eternal beings, trapped in mortal flesh, how differently would we live our lives?

At some point, I remembered the last message I had left my cousin Darla on Facebook. I sat down at the computer again and managed to finish the conversation with three simple words: *Darla, it's over.*

I knew it didn't make sense, but it was the only thought I could formulate. My hands shook so violently that it took a great deal of effort to hit "enter."

By striking that one little key, I had just told the world that my only son was no longer here.

★

Since we had lived in Florida for thirteen years and Aaron had spent nine of those in the military, only a few of our friends had enjoyed large quantities of time with him. So when the few who had known him for the full thirteen years—the few he always made time to visit when he came home—walked through my door, the pain intensified. I knew these friends understood the full measure of what I had lost...what we had all lost.

Hoss and Linda Wiggins, the friends who had hosted our anniversary celebration less than a year before, were like second parents to my boy, and their sons, Jason and Kevin, were like brothers to Aaron. We had met the Wiggins at church just after moving to Florida, and our families became fast friends. Their hearts intertwined with ours in the pride we felt over each of Aaron's achievements. They cheered our son on through every stage of his military career and prayed unceasingly through each deployment.

When Linda walked in and I fell into her arms, an entirely unexpected noise left my body. I began groaning in unbearable pain, weeping uncontrollably. If Linda was there, looking at me like she was, then the unthinkable had actually happened. Aaron was gone.

I felt life draining from my body again.

At some point, I looked out at my lawn and couldn't help but remember the times when I had driven by a similar scene and wondered what had happened and who had died. Lawns packed with vehicles in the middle of the morning only meant one thing.

I asked Hoss to lower my flag in the yard to half-mast. Something in me needed all those who passed by to know a hero had died fighting for his country. For their country.

I also needed my husband—who was still on a ferry 3,500 miles northwest of us—to find a way home.

✭

Billy

Through the kindness of strangers on the ferry and even my clients, I managed to immediately drop off the trailer for delivery and return to the loading ramp in time to catch the same ferry back. My friend Al called and told me to drive my truck straight to the Seattle airport because he and his wife had already purchased my plane ticket home. Jim, another long-time friend and previous business partner, caught a flight from Florida to Seattle so he could drive my truck back across the country to Florida.

Much later that day, I was finally in the airport sitting at my gate, when out of nowhere I heard my mother's voice. For an instant, I thought I must have been imagining things. Then my eyes focused on the TV monitor.

There, for all to see, was a picture of my boy's face.

It slowly dawned on me that somehow the reporters at CNN had already tracked down my mother in Tennessee. They had her on the phone and were showing Aaron's picture on the screen as Mom relayed the details of the last conversation she'd had with her beloved grandson.

Toward the end of the interview, I pointed up to the monitor and told the lady sitting next to me, "That's my son up there."

She said a prayer for me, and then she shared the news with several others sitting nearby. Soon, a group of people had gathered around me.

In the midst of the deepest pain I had ever experienced, I found comfort in knowing that God was not shocked by the events of the day. He knew this day would come. Our great God had *always* known that this day would come, all the way back to when Aaron was an eight-year-old boy and first decided what he wanted to do with his life.

★

Karen

That evening, Anita and Kathy, two dear friends, decided they would spend the night with me. They led me into the bedroom and told me to simply point at the clothes I would like them to pack since we would be heading to DC to be with Kimberly and the babies as soon as Billy arrived. I was overwhelmed and awed by friends who were taking charge of this situation for me…knowing I had no ability to do so for myself.

Then nighttime fell. I had no idea if I would be able to sleep. Actually, I was terrified to lie back down in that same bed where I had received the phone call from Billy fifteen hours earlier. On the other hand, I felt if I could just go to sleep, maybe tomorrow I would learn that none of it had really happened.

The house began clearing out. Adam bundled up our two grand-daughters and took them home. Ana retired to her room in exhaustion. My two friends covered up on my couches, and Tara climbed in bed with me. Lying face-to-face, she reached for my hands and held them until we both fell asleep.

Chapter Twenty

How Great Thou Art

Early the next morning, the time came to open my swollen, stinging eyes…to experience the first day of waking up in a world Aaron was no longer a part of. Tara was still lying there beside me—eyes closed—and I begged God to let me fall back to the peaceful sleep that had provided a false but comforting sense of temporary escape.

But sleep wouldn't come.

Daylight had broken. The sun had risen in the east, as if it hadn't gotten the message that Aaron was dead and time did not have my permission to move on.

It was real.

And I wanted to die.

As I dropped my legs over the side of the bed, it amazed me that I was able to stand—that my body obeyed me when it felt so empty, soulless, and utterly broken. The house was silent. Dead silent.

Hauntingly silent.

I made my way to the bathroom and there, taped to the mirror, was an index card Billy and I had previously exchanged handwritten love notes on. It hung there to remind me each morning when I woke just how blessed I was. Now it seemed to mock me—a glaring reminder of the life that was, but never would be again. I finally gained the courage to look at myself, but as expected, the face I saw was foreign to me. No expression. No feeling. Dead.

I collapsed to the counter, my body writhing. I wanted to scream, but what left my lips was a sound I had no control over, a sound I had never heard before—a breathless, agonizing, fist-clenching, silent wail.

I came to know that sound well.

I somehow summoned the energy to tidy up. It was then I noticed that I was still wearing the outfit I had worn the day before—running shorts and Aaron's brown shirt that he had received at the end of Hell Week. I didn't have the energy or presence of mind to change my clothes.

Soon after, Adam arrived to drive me to the airport. Billy was almost home. Our daughters chose to stay behind, feeling like their dad and I would need to have those first few minutes alone. What was only a thirty-minute trip to Palm Beach International Airport felt like an eternity.

As we rushed toward the concourse, Adam realized that we wouldn't be able to go through security without tickets. We would have to wait in the lounge area near baggage claim. Adam mustered the composure to calmly explain our situation to the lady at the nearest counter. With great tenderness, she walked us to security, and, without question, they sent us through to the gate where Billy would disembark.

And finally…he arrived.

Surrounded by people struggling to understand what they were witnessing, Billy and I shared a brief, wordless, gut-wrenching embrace. Then, with tear-flooded faces, and still stunned by our unspeakable new reality, we clung to each other as we made our way to the parking lot.

Walking through the terminal, I could see Aaron everywhere. We had said goodbye to him by *that* post, his backpack slung over one shoulder, sadness in his eyes. Greeted him near *that* window on another occasion, a huge smile on his face as he nearly jogged up to our waiting arms. Stopped while he bought a book in *that* shop on yet another, so he had something to read on his long flight back to Coronado.

Every step held a memory of a life that had somehow vaporized as if it had never been.

He would never come home to us again.

I finally dropped my head and practically ran for the door. Billy must have been feeling the same thing because his pace bettered mine.

After only a few minutes on the interstate, Billy told Adam and me that he would like to go straight to the church if we could stand it. In that instant, it dawned on me that it was Sunday.

Taken aback, I asked, "Are you sure?"

"Can *you* do it, Karen?"

"I can."

Adam quickly made calls to our family and friends and redirected them to meet us at Christ Fellowship's makeshift sanctuary in the Martin County High School auditorium. With me in yesterday's clothes, no make-up on, and unkempt hair, we entered a packed auditorium just as the first song began. Someone grabbed our arms and told us our family and friends were waiting down front.

We walked down the aisle to find our daughters and granddaughters along with three full rows of our dearest, closest friends here in Florida. The sight and the beautiful melody overcame me. Full band blaring, music and harmonies filling the air with the sweet sound of praise, I was completely swept into an alternate world as I heard that oh-so-familiar chorus:

> Then sings my soul, my Savior God to Thee,
> How great Thou art, how great Thou art.
> Then sings my soul, my Savior God to Thee,
> How great Thou art, how great Thou art!

That moment was as God-ordained as the sun setting in the west. We worshipped. In our utter brokenness, our deepest, most unparalleled moment of need…we worshipped. Hands thrown to the sky, shoulders shaking as tears marked our faces and melodies left our lips… we worshipped:

> When Christ shall come
> With shout of acclamation
> And take me home
> What joy shall fill my heart
> Then I shall bow
> In humble adoration
> And there proclaim
> My God, how great Thou art!

Chapter Twenty-One

Memorials and Tears

Leaving church that morning was a blur of warm hugs, tender tears, and broken-hearted prayers of comfort. Our close friends and extended community had, for the first time, witnessed up close and personal a young life willingly sacrificed on their behalf. Someone they had seen and touched. Someone they had laughed with. Someone many of them had loved.

And they felt the full weight of it.

Aaron didn't just die a tragic death. He had given his life...for them. Aaron's story of love and sacrifice was already changing people, compelling them to contemplate the worth of their lives in a different light. You could see it in their eyes as they struggled for words.

Arriving home after church, I dropped into the comfort of my chaise lounge, the one Aaron claimed as "his spot" every time he came to visit. Curling up on my right side, I remembered seeing him lie in the exact same position the last time he was home. "I love this thing. It's so comfortable. Kim, we need to get one of these when our house is built." It warmed my heart that something in my home made him feel at ease. His life was so hard, so brutal. I would have done—or purchased—anything to give him brief moments of serenity or relaxation. I pressed my face into the pillow where his face had been months earlier somehow feeling more connected to him as I matched my movements to my memory. My heart began heaving once again in unbearable pain. I would never see my boy fall onto another piece of furniture for the rest of my life…something I had watched him do for thirty years. It just couldn't be true. The realization was sinking in.

I needed to sleep. Up to that moment, sleep had been my only source of refuge.

But there was no time for sleep. Our flight north was departing soon. Billy and I, along with Tara, Ana, and Tara's family, were headed to Kimberly's parents' home. We were overcome with the *need* to be near Kimberly and the babies—near to what mattered most to Aaron. My heart was aching to hold his children in my arms and tell them everything would be okay…*somehow* everything would be okay.

Our friends realized we were overwhelmed and unable to function, so they helped us work through our flight details. They helped us finish packing and loaded our suitcases into our car. We were helplessly broken down and incapable of dealing with even the smallest tasks, so those beautiful friends literally did *everything* for us. I thank God for them each time I think back on those early days of loss.

On the flight north, I ended up with a window seat. Utterly exhausted, I leaned my swollen face against the window and closed my eyes. Billy laid his warm and comforting hand on my knee. I tried to sleep, but once again, sleep wouldn't come. Instead, in the quietness of that moment, my mind began racing, retracing my final conversations with Aaron, our final goodbye on the hotel sidewalk, the wedding vow renewal where we had all laughed so hard at his funny comment about Tara channeling my father. Unable to bare the thoughts any longer, I opened my eyes in an attempt to make the memories stop. As I gazed out the window, looking at the busy landscape below, I was suddenly overcome by the understanding of what I was looking at. It was America—the land my son had just given his life for—moving on as though nothing had happened.

And I lost it.

Billy's grip tightened on my knee, but that didn't stop the tears.

I began sobbing. It was as though this was the first moment I really acknowledged—accepted—the truth that Aaron was gone. Forever. He had really done it. He had given his life for this country. All those years of hearing him say he was willing to do just that became a reality, my reality. The sobbing grew louder.

My mind snapped back to the present when I was interrupted by the sweetest, most tender voice: "Mr. and Mrs. Vaughn, I couldn't help but notice the pain you were in. Your son-in-law just explained." Our flight attendant's eyes filled with tears as she stammered for words. "I don't know what to say, except that I am so sorry...What can we do for you? How can we help? Can we get you anything?"

I couldn't speak, so Billy answered, "No, but thank you." His voice cracked as he began breaking down.

Word spread throughout the cabin, and people began responding. Many kneeled in the aisle beside our seats and prayed over us. Someone behind me placed hands on my shoulders. I could feel them lifting my need—my agony—to God. With tears streaming down her cheeks, our flight attendant returned to place a carefully folded, handwritten note in my hand. Taking both of my hands into her own, she once again whispered, her voice cracking as she forced back tears, "I am so sorry. And I'm so grateful for your sacrifice, for your son's sacrifice, for the freedom he's given me."

As the plane touched down and began its taxi to the gate, the pilot came over the loudspeaker. "Ladies and gentlemen, we have a family onboard who's just lost a son in Afghanistan. We'd ask that you please remain in your seats and allow them to exit first."

As we walked forward, I could hear people whispering prayers over us. They were touching my hands and arms, telling me how sorry they were. It was both comforting and heartwarming. When we reached the front of the plane, the pilot took me by the arm. He escorted our family to a waiting cart completely surrounded by Continental employees. As we rode toward the pilot's lounge, I noticed a newsstand full of papers, and on the front of every single paper was a picture of Aaron's face.

"That's my son!"

The cart came to a sudden halt, and all of those beautiful people, caring for us so tenderly, just took a moment to take in the reality of what they were now a part of. A stunned silence fell over us all, broken only by the words of one of the women flanking our cart, "Oh wow…he was so handsome."

★

The following days and weeks are somewhat of a blur in my mind. Because Aaron died in a mass casualty of Navy SEALs from the famed SEAL Team VI, the story of his and his teammates' deaths was headline news for *several* days.

By Monday morning, less than 48 hours after our world fell apart, Billy and I, along with Kimberly, were Matt Lauer's guests on the Today Show. I clearly remember the mixed emotions I experienced as I did my best to fix my hair and apply makeup with arms and hands that would barely obey me. All I wanted to do was crawl into a corner, cover my head, and grieve, but I had been given a chance to tell the world about this amazing man I was privileged enough to call *my* son and I would not—I could not—discard that opportunity.

During the interview, Matt asked me, "What are you most proud of in terms of Aaron's accomplishments?"

While I found myself almost too overwhelmed to form the words, my response did not take much effort in thought. "I'm most proud of Aaron's humility and his nobility. But more than anything I'm most proud of the way he loved God and how important his faith was to him."

When the interview was over, I felt so grateful that God had given me the strength necessary to speak those words and make sure the entire world knew that Aaron was a man of faith and that he was now with Jesus.

Throughout those first few days, I continued repeating the scripture: "We do not grieve as those who have no hope, we do not grieve as those who have no hope..." (1 Thessalonians 4:13) Those words were my lifeline, my only reminder of truth in the most chaotic of circumstances. Because of my faith and Aaron's faith in Christ and the promises given in the Bible, I knew I would see Aaron again one day.

We spent the rest of Monday at Kimberly's parents home where all of Aaron's closest friends had assembled. Conversation was shallow and difficult. We were all still very much in a state of shock. And, business had to be done—decisions about Aaron's headstone and burial, insurance policies, and last wishes. Kimberly was locked away with her care officer for a large portion of that day making those unthinkable choices.

Monday was mind-numbing, but it didn't hold a candle to Tuesday.

★

On Tuesday, August 9, 2011, the bodies of those thirty American heroes returned home. Home from the battlefield they died on almost 7,000 miles away from all of us who loved them...all of us they loved.

As we entered the building at Dover Air Force Base, my eyes could barely take it in. Hundreds of strangers stood in small clusters; each cluster represented those left behind by *one* of the thirty heroes. We looked at each other with silent compassion because we could see each others' grief and wanted to help, but it wasn't as if we had anything to offer each other. We were all doing everything in our power to simply survive our own anguish.

Around the perimeter of the building were dozens of senior military officials with uniforms starched and covered with ribbons, bars, and stars. Soon President Obama entered the room, flanked by Secretary of Defense Leon Panetta, Chairman of the Joint Chiefs of Staff Admiral Michael Mullen, and many others whose names I do not recall. I quickly realized that we were in a holding room, a place to greet the dignitaries, while waiting for the staging of the transfer ceremony in a nearby air hangar. As I looked around, I noticed many unfamiliar faces of men dressed in fatigues. I later learned they were fellow members of SEAL Team VI, all of whom had flown home from Afghanistan with—and keeping watch over—their brothers' bodies.

Aaron's SEAL Team VI Chaplain spent some time with us and spoke the most amazing words, the only ones I remember from that day: "If you gave me five men like Aaron, I could conquer the world." Sometime during those first few days, Aaron's commander described him as "a fearless leader headed straight to the top." I began realizing what a powerful warrior my son had become, something I otherwise had no way of knowing since Aaron never bragged on himself or boasted over his achievements.

When the appropriate time came, the entire mass of family members was escorted to the hangar where the transfer ceremony would take place. As I turned the corner to enter the hangar, my eyes instantly focused on the largest American flag I had ever seen. It hung from the highest point of the building and stopped just over the heads of the dignitaries standing in the middle of the cold, gray, concrete floor. Just beyond that flag was a sight that almost took my knees to the ground. I actually gasped and caught Billy's arm to keep from collapsing. Several others *did* collapse at the sight.

In front of us were the open bellies of *two* C-17 military transport aircrafts, each *completely* loaded, from side to side and end to end, with American-flag-draped coffins. Words cannot adequately describe the emotional pain that ripped through my body at that sight.

We stayed in that hanger for hours as each coffin was brought from the aircraft to the center of the massive room for a slow salute of all military personnel present. After the slow salute, the coffin was slid into a transport vehicle. Once the transport vehicle held its maximum number of coffins, the doors were closed—again ceremonially—and the vehicle was driven from the premises. The President and all of the senior military leaders in attendance exited the building alongside the vehicle, another vehicle backed in, the dignitaries returned, and the process began again.

At least that's how my fragile mind remembers it.

The entire transfer ceremony took place in the confines of an eerie, awkward silence. No names were called as the coffins were brought into the hanger from the belly of the aircraft. We later learned that there was, of course, a reason for that. Most of the men had been burned beyond recognition and had not yet been identified.

★

The following weekend we held Aaron's first memorial service at the gymnasium of the high school Aaron had graduated from in Tennessee. Patriot Guard Riders—each holding large American flags—lined the entrance to the high school, and hundreds packed the gymnasium in an overwhelming show of love and respect. The greeting time after the two-hour ceremony seemed as though it would never end.

Afterward, our entire family and all of Aaron's buddies from the Teams—East and West Coast— who had attended the memorial descended on Kelly's home, which, of course, was located on the farm where we had raised Aaron...the land that had formed him...the dirt that had stained his soul. With the help of Aaron's cousins Trey and Ethan, Aaron's buddies built a fire in the ravine between Kelly's home and Granny's home. As we huddled around the fire, I heard one of Aaron's best friends say something that will always stick with me: "Aaron was a light for Christ in a *dark* world." Then an awkward silence cloaked the space as we all stood contemplating yet again just how very much we had lost.

At one point I made the mistake of glancing up the rolling hill to Granny's back porch. Suddenly all the noise surrounding me blurred into a hushed mumble as memories devoured my mind. I pictured Aaron, lying there on his belly only months earlier, teaching our granddaughter Annabelle to shoot a gun. I heard his laughter and awestruck words of excitement as Annabelle pulled the trigger and hit her target. I remembered my last conversation with him only weeks earlier in that hotel room in Virginia and recalled how I had forced myself to focus on the good time we would all have when November arrived…when we would meet back up at this farm and play on Granny's back porch.

A loud burst of laughter—from the friends and family behind me—jolted me back to the present. Aaron's buddies were drinking, and the "Aaron" stories had begun. I re-engaged, but my heart ached as I kept thinking how perfect the night would be…if only Aaron were there, too.

★

The next week we flew home to Florida and held Aaron's second memorial service. If memory serves me right, approximately 1,000 people attended that service. An overflow area had to be created after every seat was filled.

Earlier that day, as I was dressing for the service, I heard the loud roar of motorcycles nearby. Startled by the volume, I walked to our family room window to find the source. There in our driveway was a large group of Patriot Guard Riders.

When I went out to greet and thank them, a lovely woman, straddling one of the bikes, swung her leg over the engine and stood to hug me. She told me that she had lost her son over there, too. Somehow she had found the strength to now serve as our flag-bearer and escort. And once again, my heart was overwhelmed with gratitude. These incredible patriots escorted our family from our home to the service, which was held in the auditorium of the high school Aaron and Tara had attended in Florida.

As we neared the entrance, I could see two Martin County Fire Rescue ladder trucks with a massive American flag draped between them. With the sun just beginning its descent, the sight was breathtaking.

★

A few days later, we made our way north again for a memorial in Norfolk, Virginia. This was a massive event held in honor of twenty-two of the thirty men who had lost their lives in the shoot down of Extortion 17. These men were actually part of or working with SEAL Team VI—Aaron and his teammates. (The additional eight men aboard Extortion

17 were from other branches of the military and were honored by their respective commands.)

I'm sure the service was beautiful. I was simply in too much pain to process all that was happening around me. I do very distinctly remember, though, how the streets leading to the Norfolk Convention Center were lined as far as the eye could see with sailors standing at attention. My eyes still well with tears at the memory.

★

And finally, on Friday, August 26, we laid our son to rest in Arlington National Cemetery.

The immediate family members of thirteen of the men who died in the shoot down all arrived at a landing strip in D.C. We then boarded five commercial buses for the trip to the cemetery where a joint funeral would take place. A police escort led our massive convoy through the city to Arlington. Every intersection was blocked on our behalf, and the buses never stopped once.

After a brief, somewhat impersonal funeral in one of the chapels inside the gates of Arlington, we made our way out the doors into a brutally hot, clear-skied day. We filed in behind a horse-drawn caisson. Having sat in the back of the chapel, our family was the first in line for the long, agonizing walk to the burial site. (I was told the procession of people walking from the chapel to the gravesites was one mile long.) As we arrived at the burial site, we saw thirteen separate white tents pitched on lush, perfectly manicured, green grass, and in front of us lay thirteen coffins, separated from the bare dirt below them by a bright green section of turf.

The honor bestowed upon Aaron and his teammates was legendary. Dignitaries and fellow SEALs stood to the left of the coffins, rows of sailors to the right. Jets flew over in a missing man formation. A 21-gun salute pierced the silence. A folded flag was placed in my arms "on behalf of a grateful nation." And finally, the haunting melody that signified it was over...it was *really* over—"Taps."

Then came a tradition of the SEAL community that I had heard about many times from Aaron but had never witnessed. In a show of respect, the teammates of the deceased lined up and, one by one, took the Trident from their chest and pounded it—with their bare fist—into their brother's coffin. The hollow echoes of hundreds of Tridents being driven into the assemblage of coffins stretching half the length of Section 60 in Arlington National Cemetery were almost more than my broken heart could handle. I could barely look as I watched Aaron's friends, one after another after another, kneel beside his body and pay their ceremonial respects.

I distinctly remember Brad Cavner's turn. He was shaking so badly that the first punch threw his Trident off the side of the coffin. With trembling hands, he snatched it up from the earth, steadied its sharp prongs on the wooden surface, and pounded it once again with fierce determination. This time he found success. He knelt there longer than the rest, head bent low, almost as if he couldn't find the strength in his legs to stand, the strength to say goodbye to his best friend.

The pomp and circumstance finally ended, and all of the families were allowed to approach their loved one's coffin for only a few moments.

(After the funeral, many of the families, including ours, were being flown from D.C. back to Naval Air Station Oceana, the closest location to where we were being housed in an oceanfront hotel in Virginia Beach. Hurricane Irene was rapidly approaching the East Coast that day, leaving us little time to say our final goodbyes to Aaron. The flight needed to take off shortly if we were going to beat the storm.)

I watched Billy's dad, with trembling hands, slip his orange Tennessee Vols tie off his neck and then lay it along the line of Tridents covering the length of his grandson's casket. Our granddaughter Annabelle—who was five years old at the time and who loved her Uncle Aaron intensely—knelt beside that wooden box with her stuffed zebra, Jorge, tucked in her armpit. She pressed her tiny nose and lips to the space between the lower and upper halves of Aaron's casket, her delicate hands straddling the gap, and whispered her goodbye. I slipped my navy blue rubber wristband over my hand, pulled it to my chest for just a moment, kissed it, then placed it on my son's casket. I would never again need to pray for him throughout a deployment.

As the sun began to set, we all knew it was time...we had to leave. We were the only ones who hadn't returned to the transfer area.

The hardest thing I have ever forced my body to do was leave my boy's casket and walk away.

★

Less than three years later our family returned to Arlington National Cemetery for the funeral of Brad Cavner. I watched in stunned silence as Aaron's son, Reagan, with the help of an adult, punched his daddy's Trident into Brad's coffin.

Yes, the sacrifice has been great.

Part Three
The Legacy

One of many public tributes to Aaron

Chapter Twenty-Two

A Legacy of Love

ARON, WITH HIS KIND HEART, larger-than-life laughter, and crazy antics, was a hero—a world changer—to those closest to him long before he became a hero to his nation.

He was a hero to his littlest sister, Ana, whom he played with incessantly, even during his super-cool teenage years. He taught her—among many other things—how to swim, how to ride her bike, and eventually how to lay a chokehold on a would-be attacker.

He was a hero to his cousin with special needs, Hailey, whom he almost always had a protective arm around during the formative years. I am convinced God used her to make an especially strong impact on Aaron's heart, to teach him that life was unpredictable, and that perfectly functioning bodies were gifts, not a given.

He was a hero to me. His never-failing convictions kept me focused through some tough struggles. He was there for many of my saddest, most disappointing moments. God always seemed to allow Aaron to be present for the hard things, probably because he had a way of speaking life back into any dark situation.

He was a hero to his father. Aaron had grown to be more than everything Billy had prayed for in a son. He had also grown to be his friend and confidant. They shared everything: music, guns, knives, a passion for history, and an especially sacred love for Tennessee VOLS football. No matter where Aaron Vaughn was on college football Saturday—Iraq, Afghanistan, Canada, or Coronado—he and his father—if at all possible—would talk throughout the game.

And he was certainly a hero to Tara. He served faithfully as her warrior-defender, protector, and shield. They shared friends, secrets, values, beliefs, and a deep faith in Jesus Christ. Every lesson learned by one had been learned simultaneously by the other, if not through personal experience, through osmosis. Their life-long respect and admiration for one another was something to be admired. I recently found a quote that altogether characterized their lives: "Like a single soul, which dwelt in two bodies…there with me from the dawn of my memories."

To his friends, Aaron was a hero and someone they aspired to be like. I read the following comment on Facebook, shortly after Aaron's death: "Aaron was a man of honor and integrity, a man of Christ. He was a man that would do it all again if he knew the same outcome. He was a man that loved fighting for his country, his family, his friends. But, most of all, Aaron will be remembered as a man that touched lives and left his footprint in people's lives. Buddy, half of us, or if not all of us, dream of being a man of your nature, dream of being a man that you were. But we all know there is only one Aaron Vaughn, and right now he's guarding the throne room of God. Miss ya, Buddy. Love ya. See ya on the other side."

When Aaron died, a portion of each heart he had ever touched stopped beating.

★

Jamie Nail, one of Aaron's friends, shared the following story with me after Aaron's death:

"In November of 2000, Aaron and I went on a hunting trip with my granddad, Hollis Nail. Everyone, including Aaron, called him Pa. He was a solid man for his age, and I am convinced that, even at seventy-one, Pa could have whipped my butt in a wrestling match. For just about as

Aaron (left) and Jamie Nail—This photo was taken around the time Jamie lost his grandfather.

long as I remember, we would go hunting the weekend before or after Thanksgiving at Camp Blanding in Northeast Florida. In addition to being a Wildlife Management Area, this land was also a military base.

"We woke early and got about our business, but with no success. Pa suggested we move to a little out-of-the-way spot for us to finish up the afternoon and sit until sunset. We arrived at our location and prepared to head off in our own directions. As usual, we followed our same routine: a prayer, a hug, and good lucks all around. We had a rule that we would meet up after dark at the truck, and if anyone shot prior to that, everyone would just stay put until dark. Together, we'd circle up and help pull the deer out.

"So we headed off into the woods with climbing treestands on our backs. Even though we were grown men, Pa got both Aaron and I set up at our locations prior to heading off to his own. Just as dark was setting in, I heard a shot from a rifle pretty close. I knew it was from either Aaron or Pa. I did as agreed and sat until it was too dark to see through my scope and then worked myself down the tree and packed up my gear to head back to the truck. When I made it back, Aaron was waiting on me as scheduled, but Pa was nowhere around. I gave Pa another fifteen or twenty minutes and then started heading out to see if he needed help dragging out a deer.

"I searched through the areas where he should have been and could find no sign of him. That's when I started to get a little worried and started calling for him with no response.

"After an hour or so of searching, I headed back to the truck to go get help. Aaron stayed in the field where we parked in the event Pa made it out of the woods. I drove down the back roads as fast as I could to the main gate. By this time, the gate had been locked. I sat in my truck and started blowing the horn to attract the attention of some military officers across the street. Shortly, an MP (Military Policeman) arrived, and I gave him a rundown on the situation. He called up the Fish and Wildlife officers, and they arrived on the scene before too long. I guided them back to the area where I had left Aaron, and we set out on a search.

"We traveled down the same trail I had walked ten times previously, but the officer did something I had never thought to do.

"He looked up.

"As he panned up a tall pine with his light, there was Pa. I could immediately see he was no longer with us. That image will forever be etched in my mind and heart.

"The officer told me to go back and get more help. I think he was trying to protect me from what he already knew. I ran through the woods crying and growling to God for help to save my Pa.

"I made it to the field where Aaron was waiting with the other wildlife officer. Aaron grabbed me immediately. I told them we found Pa in the tree, and I had walked under him several times, never knowing he was right above my head.

"Not being certain whether Pa was still alive, Aaron held on to me and began praying over me and Pa in a way I had never seen him do before. He prayed for the Lord to touch me and comfort me. He prayed for God to touch Pa and to let him be okay.

"Not too much later, fire rescue informed me that Pa had, in fact, passed away. They pulled him down from the tree and transported him out of the woods.

"Aaron stuck by my side for the next several days and even drove Amanda, my girlfriend, across the state for the funeral.

"He was a rock for me that night and continued to be a great support afterwards. Eventually, he was a groomsman in my wedding. I still look at what he wrote on our engagement picture that everyone signed: 'Good luck for the rest of your lives, to the best match ever made. Love, Aaron.'

"Aaron was such an important part of my life while he was in it. He was a key part of events that will define who I am forever. I am so proud of him for his service to our God, families, and country. Words can never express the gratitude that I have for his sacrifice—to give up a life with his family so that I might have a life with mine.

"Aaron will forever be a part of my life and the life of every other American whether they choose to acknowledge it or not.

I love you, and I miss you, brother."

★

Many times since Aaron's death, our first-ever national television interview, the one with Matt Lauer on the Today Show, has crossed my mind. I often think about the question Matt asked, "What are you most proud of in terms of Aaron's accomplishments?" The answer I gave in the moment of utter brokenness would still be my answer today.

Here's the rest of what I said that morning: "Everything he did was secret, and it just feels really strange right now that only in his death can we celebrate who he was in his life. It's a very difficult concept to understand. *But*, what Aaron would want everybody to know most is that he loved America, he believed America could be great again, and he fought for the *America* he grew up in. We're just really sad about this huge loss. We're really sad that our son is gone. But we know, we know that…(long pause)…he would have…he would have done it all again. And he loved every minute of his life."

I thank God for men like Aaron and Brad Cavner—men who live every day as if there is no promise of tomorrow; men who understand that our freedoms and liberties must be protected and have the courage and conviction to say, "If not me, who?"; men who, at the end of their time here on earth, smile and say, "Of course I would do it all again. Heck yeah, I would *definitely* do it all again."

Aaron and Brad living the American Dream.
There was never a dull moment when these two were
together—just look at the mischief on those faces! They both
answered the call and became some of the world's most fierce war
fighters. They gave their lives so others might live.

Chapter Twenty-Three

A World Redefined

I N February 2012, six months after Aaron's death, *Act of Valor* was released in theaters across America. Kimberly and the babies were visiting with us in Florida at the time. I remember looking around our family room on opening night and asking everyone, "Can we do this?"

We all knew it was something we *had* to do.

For Aaron.

Our sense of dread was almost palpable as our entire family entered the Regal Cinemas at the Treasure Coast Mall in Jensen Beach—yet another place vividly marked by dozens of "Aaron" memories.

We took our places against the back wall, as if distance from the screen might protect our fragile hearts when he finally appeared. We had no idea when to expect to see him since he wasn't there to tell us.

So we waited.

We kept glancing at each other through different scenes, whispering, "Was that him?"

"I don't know. I don't think so…"

"There? Is that…"

"No, doesn't look like his body."

Suddenly there he was—in full living color. I thought my heart would stop. Kimberly grabbed my arm—fingers digging into my skin. We both gasped. Aaron jumped out of a black rubber raft and ran straight toward the screen. Straight toward *us*.

As he ran past the camera, we then saw him from the rear, headed toward a building the SEALs were about to raid. I would have known his body anywhere. That stride was so familiar. For just a moment, I was back in front of our old house, street marked at forty yards from the edge of the driveway, timing his speed, rebuilding the knee.

I wanted to look away, but I knew I would regret it if I did.

In real life and now in this film, Aaron was a lead breacher—the door kicker. He flipped around as he reached the building's entrance, SEALs flanking him in every direction. As he nodded to his teammates that it was time to go, the camera zoomed in for a close-up of his beautiful blue eyes and strong, square jaw.

And then, in a moment's flash, he was gone.

✯

On August 6, 2011, the sacred was torn from our lives.

Aaron's death redefined our entire family. It set us on a path I never dreamed we would be forced to walk. The road to healing is long. Actually, it is never-ending. There's great truth in the statement, "Just because you get through something doesn't mean you get over it."

We expected Aaron to be sitting at our table as we aged, laughing with his sisters about all the fun years of growing up, telling and re-telling wild tales about his years as a Navy SEAL, and recounting the story to Reagan and Chamberlyn of how he met their mother that beautiful night in Guam.

We expected to sit beside Aaron and Kimberly on the bleachers for Reagan's first football game. We laughed about what it would be like in the Vaughn home when Chamberlyn brought home her first boyfriend. We longed to watch our son relish in the joys of raising a family of his own. And we prayed they would bring him even half the joy he brought us.

But God had a different plan.

★

We will miss Aaron till the day we die. We'll grieve his absence. We'll long for his laughter. His stocking will hang between mine and Tara's (in order of birth) during every Christmas season as long as we live. We'll never again gather as a family without aching for that missing face…the missing smile…the missing laughter.

But we will carry on—thankful that we had him in our lives. Knowing that one glorious day we will all be together again.

This time forever.

And God shall wipe away all tears from their eyes;
and there shall be no more death, neither sorrow, nor crying,
neither shall there be any more pain.
~ Revelation 21:4

Aaron was posthumously awarded the Purple Heart, the Defense Meritorious Service Medal, and the Bronze Star Medal with "V" for Valor. His additional decorations include: Joint Service Achievement Medal with "V" for Valor, Presidential Unit Citation, National Defense Service Medal, 2 Sea Service Deployment Ribbons, Navy Expert Rifleman Medal, Navy Expert Pistol Shot Medal, 2 Navy and Marine Corps Achievement Medals (1 with "V" for Valor), Combat Action Ribbon, 2 Navy Good Conduct Medals, Iraq Campaign Medal, Afghanistan Campaign Medal, Global War on Terrorism (Service) Medal, Global War on Terrorism (Expeditionary) Medal and numerous other personal and unit decorations.

The Legacy
of a Life Well-Lived

I REMEMBER SITTING IN A Beth Moore Bible Study about two months after Aaron died. Beth's video lesson that night focused on the Israelites' fear of actually crossing over into the promised land after having wandered in the desert for forty years. At the end of the lesson, Beth asked us to close our eyes and picture ourselves standing in the middle of the Jordan River. She explained that the middle represented the place of indecision—the place where one of two options must be chosen. We can either go back to what we know (our place of comfort, even if it's an ugly place) or else move forward into the potentially frightening but possibly magnificent new land.

As I followed Beth's instructions, I closed my eyes and visualized myself standing in the middle of the river, which was parted just like it had been for the ancient Israelites. I noticed that the ground beneath my feet was damp from the river's water that now stood still on either side of me. I paused for a moment before looking toward the river bank ahead of me—the promised land, the land God had prepared for me and prepared me for. The next moment, I lifted my eyes and saw Aaron standing on that bank, smiling at me with his huge grin that was so warm and so reassuring. He began enthusiastically waving me over with his right hand while his left hand rested on his knee, as if he was positioning himself to help me up the bank as soon as I came near enough. I could barely contain myself when I heard him call out to me, "Mom! Just walk. Come on, walk, Mom! You can do it!"

In the years since Aaron's death, I've wondered over and over again how this small-town girl, who lived on a farm in Northwest Tennessee, ended up where I am now. As I think through the opportunities and challenges, I believe I know the answer—I stayed on my feet, and I kept walking.

Looking back, I can see how God delicately and intentionally equipped me with every tool I would need to fulfill His new call on my life. He always knew this day would come and was not taken by surprise. He had a plan. And all He wanted from me was a heart that would say "yes" to whatever He requested next. I've shaken my head in wonder as I've walked through unimaginably huge doors of opportunity seemingly kicked open by God Himself.

I've often said that the day Aaron's life ended mine began again. Let me explain. Within hours after Extortion 17 was shot down, social media exploded with many questions, fair questions, from thousands of Americans. "Why were so many SEALs on a single helicopter? Why was America's most elite unit flying into a hot landing zone in an old, antiquated chopper built in the 1960s?"

Many questions and so few answers. Billy and I both struggled to understand exactly what went wrong on that fateful night. In the midst of our quest to understand what had happened, and why, we left the comfort and security of our home to start fighting for those who were fighting for us. We sought transparency and answers for the many questions that haunted us day and night. What lay ahead was potentially frightening, but we knew we had to say "yes" to each open door that our quest might take us through.

The media embraced our efforts and began giving us air time to talk about the issues our search uncovered. We wrote a book, *Betrayed: The Shocking True Story of Extortion 17,* and spent every cent we had touring the country and sharing our story of newfound concern and grave personal loss.

Aaron's exemplary life made our story compelling and forced good people out of their chairs and into our cause. Social media platforms exploded again, but this time with support for our efforts. We began writing OpEds targeting the issues our search brought to light, and we asked military families and everyday citizens to engage alongside us.

After dozens of appearances on major news outlets, Billy and I became somewhat of a voice for Gold Star[1] families across America and were called upon regularly to speak about the hardships our warfighters were experiencing in the longest war in America's history. I also received requests to speak in high schools, talking to students about the sacrifices made by tough men and women willing to give everything for our nation's safety and security.

In late 2013, I was offered an advisory role with Concerned Veterans for America and began touring the nation on their "Defend Freedom Tour." For the next three years, I shared that massive platform with giants for freedom like Oliver North, Allen West, Sean Parnell, and Pete Hegseth, reaching thousands upon thousands with Aaron's story of sacred sacrifice and selfless service.

In 2016 I had the unexpected honor of speaking during a primetime slot on the opening night of the Republican National Convention, where over thirty million people heard me describe Aaron's great love for this country and my unwavering passion to continue fighting culturally the battle my son had fought kinetically.

---

[1] *Gold Star Mother...what does that mean?*

During World War I, families of soldiers hung flags or banners in the windows of their homes. These flags included a blue star for every immediate family member serving in the conflict. If one of those family members died in the war, a gold star was sewn over the blue to indicate to all passing by that a member of that family had paid the ultimate sacrifice. The tradition continues today.

OUR FREEDOM
has now been bought by the blood of a childhood friend...
Naval Special Warfare Operator (SEAL)

Chief Petty Officer
AARON CARSON VAUGHN
Seal Team 6

DOB: June 24, 1981
Walked with God on August 6, 2011

OCCHS Class of 1999
OCCHS Rebel Football #1

I have fought a good fight,
I have finished my course,
I have kept the faith.
2 Timothy 4:7

Some of Aaron's high school friends had this plaque made just after Aaron's death.
It hangs on a wall inside Hillcrest Elementary School in Troy, Tennessee.

Billy and I have been given a tremendous platform, and we understand—with every heartbeat—the intense responsibility that comes with it. Our son gave his final breath for its creation. Even if we wanted to (and there are many times we have), we couldn't *go back* to life as we knew it. We have a mission and believe that we have been placed in this position, with this unique perspective, for a purpose. So we keep walking forward.

Our public journey has led many Americans to know our boy, but Aaron's notoriety came *long* before ours. Our interview with Matt Lauer, in addition to the interview Billy's mother gave CNN on the morning we learned of Aaron's death, threw Aaron's name and face into a spotlight that we had no idea was in the making. Because Aaron lived a life of such honor and nobility, his death began changing hearts across this nation... hearts of men and women whom he had never met. His legacy began changing the world he had left behind.

Over the years, thousands of letters have flooded our mailboxes—physical and electronic—from Americans and from people from other nations as well explaining that Aaron's story has changed them forever. Many told us they have given their life to Christ after learning the depth of Aaron's faith. Others wrote to say they were inspired to give their marriage, career, or friendships a fresh look after witnessing Aaron's example of a life so well-lived.

Aaron's tattoo

Many wrote to say they have chosen a life of service in order to honor Aaron's sacrifice. Dozens of men—and a few women—told us that they wanted to duplicate Aaron's "Molon Labe" tattoo that had somehow become iconic.

Today, many little boys bear Aaron's name. They are the sons of his SEAL teammates, the son of his best friend from high school, Will David Coleman, whom Aaron reconnected with in Nashville during his last year on earth, and the sons of people who never knew Aaron but heard his story. These parents have told Billy and I that their children will know Aaron. They'll know about his character. They'll know about his intense goodness. And they'll know about his sacrifice. I have to believe in my heart that these kids will grow up seeing America in a different light than most and will become world changers themselves.

In our hometown of Stuart, Florida, just outside the gate of the local water park, stands a memorial dedicated to Aaron. It serves as a blazing reminder to every family who enters that their freedom to enjoy the beauty and fun in that park was paid for in blood by a young man who lived right in their backyard. I've heard that many teachers stop at the monument and tell their students about Aaron before entering the park for their class trips. In addition, not far off the coast of Martin County, Florida, is the Aaron Vaughn Memorial Reef (Lat. N27 12.785', Lon. W80 05.610'), named in his honor by a unanimous vote of local officials.

Another memorial to Aaron stands near the athletic fields of Obion County Central High School in Troy, Tennessee. Its inscription, written by his classmates, is still tender to my soul even though I've read it a thousand times: "Our freedom has now been bought by the blood of a childhood friend." For generations, high school students will be researching this hometown hero who left this earth in a blaze of fearless glory and will know that he, too, was once just like them.

Each June, approximately 300 open-water swimmers descend on our small beach-front town to swim in the Aaron Vaughn Memorial Frogman Swim (a 1K or 5K open water ocean swim held with all proceeds going to Operation 300). Each fall hundreds of motorcyclists hit Abernathy's Harley Davidson in Union City, Tennessee, for the Annual Aaron Vaughn Memorial Ride to remember him, to honor him, and to thank him.

Every year on August 6, the men and women from our nearest fire rescue station pull their ladder trucks and ambulances to the front of our home to pay their respects and to place a boot full of flowers at the base of our flagpole. On any given day you can pull into the Martin County Sheriff's office and find multiple SWAT Team members wearing a T-shirt with Aaron's name on it. You can circle the parking lot and spot dozens of vehicles marked with a simple logo our family created bearing two letters: AV. Something about Aaron's story has captured our local law enforcement and fire rescue teams, and it drives them to be better, to work harder, and to refuse failure in whatever task lies before them.

And then there's Operation 300. After Aaron's death, we heard Kimberly—with an utterly broken heart—speak the following words many times: "Who's going to teach my children the things their father would have taught them?" As we considered Kimberly's question, it wrecked us,

Good Housekeeping published an article
about Tara and Operation 300 in July 2015.

Tara and Aaron

but at the same time it gave birth to a dream. Tara had been searching for a way to honor her brother's life and in 2012 she left her full time job and founded—with Billy by her side as co-founder—Operation 300.

Operation 300 is a nonprofit organization that hosts weekend adventure camps for children who lost their fathers in service to our country. These children are paired one-on-one with father-aged male mentors, and they have the time of their lives participating in activities they might have done with their dads. We also bring the moms in to spend the weekend relaxing in one of the luxury hotels in South Florida. So much good has come from this organization. Hundreds of volunteers give of their time throughout the year to be part of these incredible weekends, helping these children laugh again, play again, and be a kid again. And all of this hard work is dedicated to the legacy of the man who changed us all…Aaron Vaughn.

On and on the list could go. Aaron's name has become synonymous with patriotism, courage, grit, and fearlessness—just like his daddy had hoped for all those many years before when he held his tiny baby to his chest. The tapestry woven by Aaron's intensely principled life has become a massive work of art, changing people, changing environments, and changing this world. He left the world better than he found it. Oh, if we all could do the same.

I am so proud of all Aaron was and the way his life continues to inspire people to become better versions of themselves: givers rather than takers, encouragers, builders, uplifters of the broken hearted, and people who truly see the needs of others and boldly—selflessly—reach into their lives to help.

And me? I am going to continue walking forward. I am devoted to leaving a legacy of my own now. I am trying every day to live a life that really matters, a life my daughters, my sons-in-law, and my grandchildren will be proud of and will remember me fondly for when I am no longer here. I want to live a life worthy of the tremendous sacrifice that has been made on my behalf. I want to seize every day, draining every drop of substance and worth from the minutes and hours between dawn and nightfall.

In other words…I want to live like Aaron.

"Therefore…, since we are surrounded by so great a cloud of witnesses, let us lay aside every weight, and the sin which so easily ensnares us, and let us run with endurance the race that is set before us, looking unto Jesus, the author and finisher of our faith…"
~ Hebrews 12:1-2 (NKJV)

Study Guide

By Karen Vaughn & Tara Baldwin

★

I realize not everyone will read the following chapters simply because Aaron's part of the story is over, and that's okay. If you choose to stop here, I challenge you to think about Aaron's life and consider how you can best raise your children to leave a positive mark on our world. Sometime today or during an upcoming weekend, sit down with your children and type Aaron's name into the search box on your phone or computer. Show your children who Aaron was. Tell them some of the stories I told you. Laugh with them about his courage to punch White Cow in the face and allow their eyes to well with tears and their hearts to fill with gratitude as you tell them how this one man—so full of love and life—placed their lives above his and fought and died to keep them safe and free.

Introduction

How do you know if you are parenting properly? How do you know if your child will be a world changer and leave a legacy you can be proud of? How do you raise a child with integrity, character, grit, and strength?

As Billy and I have traveled around the country sharing Aaron's story over the past several years, countless parents have asked us those very questions and hundreds more like them. This Study Guide is simply my response to those hundreds of questions we have received. Hopefully, it will give you some insight into how Billy and I raised Aaron, Tara, and Ana and what we taught them during their formative years. As I pondered exactly what to share in this section, I sat down with Tara who is busy raising a small part of the next generation of America. We talked about what her father and I did right as well as what we could have done better. We navigated through the parenting skills that she's adapted, and together we processed which skills she believed were most pertinent to raising strong, independent, courageous children. We also discussed how to practically apply those skills in everyday life. What you're about to read is a labor of love between a mother and her grown daughter. I'm truly honored that you've chosen to take this journey.

Let's dig in.

★

Wouldn't it be wonderful if there was a secret formula for perfect parenting? Because, let's face it, this is one seriously difficult job. We spend *every* ounce of our energy guiding, training, and instructing these beautiful blank canvases whom we were blessed enough to give birth to or adopt. Parenting is exhausting work, but we keep pushing forward because in our hearts we *know* it's worth it.

We also spend immeasurable amounts of time worrying, praying, and hoping they'll turn out *good*, turn out *right*. Unfortunately, children don't come with manuals, and yet there will never be another *anything* placed in our arms that has more value or that creates a more intense sense of responsibility than our children. I told both of my daughters, when each of them gave birth to their first child, "Welcome to the world of guilt. You'll never feel sufficient again." Laughable but true.

As parents, we invest so much in our children. We willingly—and joyously—surrender our best, most productive years to our kids, caring much more deeply about *their* needs than our own.

Changing diapers and holding bottles, endless rocking and sleepless nights, trips to the doctor for ear infections or sports injuries?

Check.

Pinching pennies to make sure they have everything they need?

Of course.

Three meals a day year after year, endless taxi rides to and from school, social events, or sports activities?

We don't think twice.

Once our kids reach a certain age, many of us will spend half our existence sitting on the sidelines of some kind of practice. And we'll do it with no regret because we know our example will teach our children to offer the same type of support to their children one day.

We listen to their dreams and ache through every defeat. If it's midnight when they tell us they need to talk, and even though we have to be up at the crack of dawn, we sit down on the side of that bed and listen. First, because we love them, and second, because we want to model before them what we pray they'll be to their stressed-out or broken-hearted child one day.

We forgive *them* so they'll learn to forgive *others*. (That is a trait they'll need in order to live fruitful lives.)

We praise and encourage them so they will be confident adults, willing and able to praise and encourage others.

It is *all* about *their* future. Every bit of it.

Parenting *is* hard, but it's also temporary.

We know the day will come when we release these infinitely unique creatures God blessed us with into adulthood. Prayerfully, it will be a moment of great pride. *Look what we've given you, world. This is our gift to you! This will be our legacy.*

The Word Is "No"

Don't be afraid to use it.

REMEMBER HOW I TOLD YOU about Aaron's allergies as a child and how cuddly and adorable he was due to that long-unidentified condition? He was so easy to love, so easy to say "yes" to. All he had to do was look up at me with those huge blue eyes and I would have given him the moon if I could have roped it.

"Yes, sweetie. You want that cookie? Let mommy get it for you. Yes, yes, yes, yes."

And then he turned two.

A new word hit my vocabulary.

"NO! Don't touch that, sweetie! It will give you a boo-boo."

"Nooooo, Teddy Ruxpin didn't need a bath, baby. Especially not in the toilet! Oh no, no, no, no...don't put him in your mou...ugh."

All of us are comfortable saying "no" during our children's toddler years when its use clearly prevents an inevitably bad situation. So why do so many of us struggle with its use as our children move up in years? Does it still not serve the same purpose?

I admit that it's hard telling your teenager they can't go somewhere or do something when your heart is aching to give them what they want, aching to say "yes." We say "no" because we know that what they ask for, no matter how innocent it appears, is not good for them. It is our job, no matter how painful, to be the "bad guy" and to keep our children safe and pure. It is taxing work. And it is hard, but it is necessary.

Remember, it's good to be our children's friend, but being their parent should always take priority.

Be tough. Don't cave. Lead them.

Questions

1. Can you think of a time you said "yes" to your children when you knew you should have said "no"?

2. What were the consequences?

3. Do you ever feel manipulated by your children? If so, how do you respond when they turn up the pressure?

4. What practical steps can you put in place to make sure you're not allowing yourself to be manipulated into saying "yes" when you know the answer should be "no"?

Discipline
It's not a dirty word.

Most of us tend to think about discipline as something that is very negative. Yet, according to the *Merriam-Webster Dictionary*, which defines discipline as "training that corrects, molds, or perfects the mental faculties or moral character," discipline is actually one hundred percent positive. (And who doesn't want a child with perfect mental faculties and moral character?)

Many perceive discipline as negative because the word is often used synonymously with punishment. That misperception causes a lot of parents to fear discipline. However, when discipline is interpreted and applied correctly, it is simply the training necessary to correct an area in a person's life. A serious consequence might be incorporated as part of that training, as illustrated below, but discipline itself is positive and a necessity in life.

Here's a key to great parenting—we need to be deliberate in making sure our children understand that discipline is not our choice but rather our obligation. What do I mean by that? When rules and the consequences for breaking those rules are clearly set, the outcome of breaking a rule is between the rules and the rule breaker, not the rule breaker and the parent. "You knew what the rule was. You made the choice for both of us. Now I'm left with no choice, and I have to follow through with the consequence I promised." At this point, the structure of the follow-through is critical. This is where the rubber meets the road—whatever you told them would happen if they broke the rules, make sure it actually happens and that it happens swiftly. When you don't follow through, it's not an act of grace but rather an affirmation that "my mom and dad don't mean what they say."

And disrespect begins.

Always remember—inaction *IS* action.

We love our children, so we follow through knowing that their lives would be a mess without discipline—the primary action that stands between a wrecked life and a productive one. We want our kids to succeed, so we do what has to be done. Disciplining our children consistently and effectively is an exasperating, never-ending struggle, but when we slack off in this particular area, we've done a disservice not only to our children but also to their future families, to their future employers, and to society in general. No pressure there, mom and dad!

True freedom is impossible without a mind made free by discipline.
~Mortimer J. Adler

Questions

1. Is discipline hard for you? If so, why?

2. Do you consistently follow through with the predetermined consequences of rule-breaking?

3. What are the potential outcomes of failing to follow through?

4. What are the benefits of fair and consistent discipline?

5. Do you think it's fair to say that a lack of discipline is a disservice to a child?

Don't Spock It Up
Are we getting this right?

MANY YEARS AGO A FATHER came to my husband asking for advice on how to handle his out-of-control child. The boy had kicked his mother in a shoe store when she refused to dish out big money for a pair of sneakers the child felt he deserved. You can imagine my husband's reaction.

Unfortunately, that scenario is an all-too-common problem in our current society. As my mother once put it, "Dr. Spock screwed us all!" (If you're too young to be familiar with Dr. Spock, all you really need to know is that he basically instructed more than one generation of young mothers to allow their children to essentially rule the roost. He instructed us to treat our children like adults.) The idea that a child deserves to be treated like an adult is ludicrous. They are not adults. They don't think like adults. They don't process consequences like adults. And if we love them—and I know we all do—it is our most serious responsibility to train them. Yes, *train* them by implementing good, solid, consistent constraints and boundaries.

I can promise you this: nine times out of ten, a child who is left to himself, allowed to make his own decisions about what he will and will not do, will be an utter failure as an adult.

And may I also add…children *desire* rules. They perform better, feel better, and behave better when their parents provide them with structure. Structure breeds security. Security breeds emotional health. Emotional health breeds well-developed, capable adults.

But on a lighter note, sometimes our kids do things for which we know we need to enforce consequences, but wow, what they did was truly hilarious. I mean journal-entry funny.

Aaron and Ana

We, of course, taught our children not to have a sassy mouth or to talk back to us in a disrespectful way. They knew without a doubt that was an absolute "no-no" in our house. One night at the dinner table, Billy was scolding Ana who was about five at the time. When he finished pointing out what she'd done that had upset him, she blurted out in a very sarcastic tone, "So?"

As soon as the syllable left her mouth, she knew she had made a big mistake. Everyone at the table instantly stopped what they were doing to see how Billy would react.

With a stern tone, Billy said, "Ana, *what* did you just say to me?"

Using the sweetest, most sing-song voice imaginable, Ana replied, "I said…(long pause as she searched for the right response)…so…ey?"

"Who's Soey?" Billy couldn't help but laugh.

Ana has never lived that one down. That tale has surfaced in the "funny moments" stories nearly every time we walk down memory lane.

Understand that there are times when it's okay to just laugh. Enjoy those moments.

But at the same time, never compromise your responsibility to develop their character by overlooking problems that you *know* need correcting.

Questions

1. Can you recall a time when your child broke the rules and you could barely contain yourself from laughing out loud?

2. How did you manage the balance between correcting the behavior and appreciating the humor in the situation?

3. What do you think the difference is between character and behavior?

4. Do your children adhere to the guidelines you set? Why or why not?

Love Well, Live Well
What's love got to do with it?

L ET'S BE HONEST. MOST KIDS don't come into this world as darling little cherubs who never misbehave, throw tantrums, or unbutton your entire shirt in public when you're not paying attention. (Yes, that really happened!) They enter this world as completely selfish, demanding, little humans. They don't know any better. And if left to themselves, they will grow up to be completely selfish, demanding, big humans.

That's why God gives us parents.

I saw a poster many years ago that read "God loves me just the way I am, but too much to let me stay that way." That is exactly how good parents see their children.

Unfortunately, many of us have been bamboozled—by media, movies, self-help books, and other sources—into believing our kids will be what they will be and it's our job to simply protect them as they mysteriously "become." That's not love, my friend, and as a result, we're watching society crumble before our eyes.

I shudder as I contemplate the generation of kids who have now hit college and need "safe spaces" to avoid hearing opinions they disagree with. Where do you think that started? Let's not become so sophisticated and enlightened that we no longer teach good common sense.

One clear result of today's illogical thinking is the explosion of stories about teachers who are verbally and physically abused by their students. And then, in the aftermath, we hear the so-called "parent" defending the child's actions. How is that good for anybody?

Teach your children respect, and they'll be respectful. Teach them love, and they'll be loving. Teach them tolerance, and they'll be tolerant toward others. Teach them to be kind, and the doors of this world will fling open in their presence.

Questions

1. Do you believe children are born with the ability to be selfless? Or is that trait learned? If so, how?

2. How do children learn to love?

3. How do children learn to appreciate their loved ones? Do you believe that just happens naturally?

4. Is it important that your children learn to love others more than themselves? Why or why not?

5. Are you teaching your child to love well or poorly? How?

6. What role does love play in teaching our children to respect the relationships they are in, including their relationships with us?

Building Your Tribe
Does it really take a village?

John Kuebler had it right: "Show me your friends, and I'll show you your future." The importance of the community we choose to raise our children in cannot be overstated.

When we actively seek relationships with families that share our values and other commonalities, we are literally creating a "tribe" in which our children can learn, grow, and thrive. The people surrounding us are not simply our friends. In our children's minds, those people are the ones we see "fit" to have a place in our lives. Or, in other words, if a child is seeking to please you, he may very well pick up the traits of those in whom you seem to be pleased.

As I think back to those years of raising our kids, I see a marked difference in the ease of raising Aaron and Tara compared to raising Ana. I contribute that difference primarily to the fact that Aaron and Tara were raised with a tribe. They were surrounded not only by our friends but also by our family: great-grandmothers, grandparents, aunts, uncles, cousins, great-aunts and great-uncles. Even after our church split and the loss of so many close friends, we made new friends—with shared values—in our new church. Aaron and Tara were forced by nature to live under a deep sense of accountability. No matter where they turned, someone was watching. In addition, because we raised them in a tribe of people who shared our values, Aaron and Tara grew up playing with children whose parents placed the same restrictions on them as we placed on our kids. Their friends were held to the same standards as they were, creating a sense of normalcy for what we taught as "good behavior." That value cannot be underestimated.

Ana wasn't quite as fortunate to be raised in that type of community, and rearing her, in all honesty, was much more difficult. I think that difficulty was due in part to the fact that we moved to Florida when Ana was only five, and she never had a tribe, that circle of accountability like Aaron and Tara had. We were a little older when we adopted Ana, so in our new circle of friends, who were our age, no one had a child Ana's age. All of their children were in their teens or older. (After moving to Florida, I prayed many times for friends with children Ana's age, but unfortunately, that prayer was never granted.) As Ana forged her way into her teenage years, she had a lot of anonymity and very little accountability because the city of Stuart was much bigger than our small hometown in Northwest Tennessee. She struggled against our rules in great part because no one in her circle of friends was held to as high of a standard as we placed on her.

Believe me, your tribe matters.

If your tribe doesn't reflect the values you want to pass on to your kids, work earnestly to build a different one. I promise that it will make your parenting much less stressful.

Questions

1. Do you have a tribe?

2. If not, what's keeping you from having this type of support system?

3. If so, how did that tribe come to be? Did you actively and intentionally build it?

4. Does your current tribe reflect your personal values?

5. What steps have you taken/can you take to build the kind of tribe you desire?

The Value System
Mission Accomplished?

"You have to know what you believe and *why* you believe it." If my children heard that phrase once, they heard it a hundred times. We wanted to make sure that the values we drove into their hearts throughout their childhood were based on truths that would not fail them—truths they could rely on when confusion or doubt came clawing at their minds. I firmly believe that this is why Aaron never rode the fence on issues.

Our family values—our expectations—were very well outlined and provided a standard we expected our kids to live up to. After all, we reminded them that every time they walked out our door they were representing our name. We have artwork above our front door that reads "Return with Honor."

By teaching them truth and living out our value system before them, we inadvertently taught them to trust us. My last Mother's Day card from Aaron is locked away in my safe—it's a treasure of unspeakable value. One line reads "I've never trusted anyone as much as I trust you."

When our kids became adults, we didn't need to beg them to treat us with respect. They treated us with respect because we had earned it by being consistently trustworthy and consistently principled enough to live out in our lives what we expected them to live out in theirs. Do as I say, but not as I do? No. Your words don't mean any more to your child than they mean to you.

Questions

1. How much of an influence do you believe society has on shaping your child's values?

2. Do your kids understand and share your values?

3. Does your family have a mission statement (a clear description of who you are and what you find important)?

4. How can you daily reinforce the values you hope to pass on to your children? Think of some practical examples.

5. How are you living out your value system in front of your children? Can you say to them "watch how I ..."?

Fear

Is it defining you?

I'T'S HARD TO BELIEVE HOW dangerous our society has become, isn't it? I never imagined it would be like this by the time my grandchildren entered the world. Through technology alone, our next generation has access to unthinkable dangers. My friend, former Army Ranger and New York Times bestselling author Sean Parnell, often says, "We have more technology in our back pockets these days than it took to put a man on the moon." So true and so frightening, especially when that technology is placed in the hands of our little blessings whose temporal lobes are just starting to develop.

How much technology to expose children to, at what age is it appropriate, and what types of safeguards to use are hot topics in parenting groups and online forums. We fear the harms that technology can do, and we seek a way to protect our kids from it. However, my focus in this lesson is not necessarily on the dangers of technology, but rather simpler issues—scenarios that are frightening but necessary for the development of strong, independent, empowered children.

When I was a child, my mother allowed my brother and me to ride our bikes to a service station about three miles away. We would make a morning of it. I can't imagine how much courage it took for my mom—who worked in the hospital and was constantly exposed to tragic accidents—to allow us to spend an entire morning riding on the roads by ourselves. I imagine she checked on us many times without our knowledge. Despite whatever fear she felt in letting us go alone, it made us feel so grown-up, and it encouraged our sense of responsibility and independence.

I realize most of us can't allow such a situation in our current society, but there *are* age-appropriate allowances of freedom and independence that we can give our kids if we spend some time thinking it through. Think back to the dangers of technology. We set up safeguards, time limits, rules, and boundaries for our kids to use their electronic devices. And we allow our children to freely play on those devices as long as they stay within our restraints. We do this because society tells us technology is acceptable, even if we fear its dangers. We need to carry over that same mindset to all aspects of our children's lives and allow them to have age-appropriate freedoms and independence, all within an environment structured by our boundaries.

Children must be allowed to experience risk. They must be allowed—on their own—to overcome challenges. They must learn to deal with and handle fear. If we block these important steps of growth, we may very well be crippling our children's entire future—something no parent wants.

As you contemplate the questions below, assess whether or not your everyday fears are reasonable. Figure out where you might be able to let go and allow growth while managing a healthy ratio of safety to risk.

Questions

1. On a scale of 1-5, 1 being "not that concerned" and 5 being "I'm losing sleep over it," how fearful are you on a daily basis regarding your child's physical safety and wellbeing?

2. At your child's current state of development, what are your biggest fears?

3. Do you find yourself allowing irrational fear to limit your child's freedom to explore, act independently, or make his or her own decisions?

4. What are some ways you might allow your child a greater level of independence while taking an acceptable amount of risk?

The Fixer
When a Band Aid's not enough

VERY FEW THINGS CAUSE MORE stress than watching our children experience emotional or physical pain. When the injury or offense is something we are completely powerless over, our sense of helplessness is equally overwhelming. And, as our children grow in age, so grows the seriousness and intensity of their problems.

I think the mothers reading this might agree with me that we have a tendency to rush in and try to "make it all go away." We can't bear to see our precious children in pain, so we do our best to find a patch or an instant cure. Sometimes we offer platitudes and then pretend the situation never happened because we can't stay in that state of stress too long.

The problem with instant cures and platitudes is that a wound must endure a process in order to heal properly. A scar doesn't form on our body moments after we suffer an injury. First, we apply pressure to stop the bleeding until the blood has time to clot. After that, a scab begins to form. If we pick at that scab, we're going to reopen the wound. We can and *should* do certain things to aid the healing, but ultimately we have to keep our hands off of it and let the process do its job. The scar is the *final* phase.

Over the course of my life, I've learned to love scars. Scars have stories. Scars are deep and solid...immovable. Really big scars prove that something tried to take us out but we had the final say. And last but not least, when we scratch a scar, it doesn't bleed. It's been down that road before and has built a barrier between the tender vessels within and the affliction without.

Fight the urge to wrap up your child's pain in a neat little package with a bow on top. Healing is going to take some time. It took years for Aaron and Tara to completely heal from the emotional devastation caused by our church split. As their parent, I could have swept their grief under the rug, dismissing the magnitude of their loss, but I didn't. Instead I let them talk to me about it as often as they needed to and as many times as they needed to. I let them heal on their timeline and didn't insist that they heal on mine. I didn't see their grief as an inconvenience to me; I saw it as something they needed time to deal with and something that needed time to develop its scar.

Try to find a way to remain calm and encouraging as you walk beside your children through their pain until the scars form.

Questions

1. Have you ever tried to make light of a problem in order to bypass the hard conversations?

2. Have you ever watched your child experience something difficult and you didn't have the answer? How did you handle that?

3. In these situations, how can you champion optimism over defeat?

4. Have you ever rushed to fix a situation that *couldn't* be fixed?

5. Have you ever been in a situation where you watched your child endure pain, wishing you could do something to take it away, only to realize later that it was something he or she needed to experience?

Shelter Free Zone
No pain, no gain

Unfortunately, emotional pain is an inevitable part of life. It comes at our kids in many forms: hurtful words from a classmate; betrayal by a friend and confidant; no invitation to the big birthday party "everyone else" has been invited to; broken relationships that ended poorly; or getting cut from a team they really wanted to be a part of. We must equip our children with the skills and mentality necessary to deal with and overcome these potentially crippling blows. For *their* sake, not ours.

Parachuting in to right every wrong on a child's behalf can actually rob him of the valuable lessons he needs to experience in order to prepare him for a successful life. Our kids *must* learn, under our careful tutelage, how to work through difficulties. Don't let the opportunities be wasted—every hurtful experience has a take-away and becomes an opportunity for growth. Those teachable moments are when our relationships with our children will be real, powerful, and life-giving. Think of it this way: When do you seek help? When do you seek wisdom? Is it in the good times or in the bad? Embrace the truth that our children's hearts are just like ours.

You and I have no idea what troubles may lie in wait for these kids we love so much. We need to prepare them to be strong and to be able to stand when everything around them is pushing them to the ground.

Teaching them these skills could very well be their salvation one day.

Ana was eighteen years old when Aaron was killed. *Seven weeks later* her long-term boyfriend Jason was killed in a car accident. I'll never forget the shrieks of horror piercing the quiet morning as she received the news from Jason's mother. I ran from my bedroom to find her collapsed on Billy's shoulder screaming hysterically, "He's dead, he's dead." That's more than any one person should have to endure in a lifetime much less in a seven-week span.

But almost six years later, Ana is still on her feet. She's still moving forward. Because she's strong.

Tara, after enduring the horrific loss of her brother, could have secluded herself in a world of grief. Instead she opened herself up and began Operation 300. *She* chose to *give back* to others who were suffering through the loss of a loved one. *Her* love and strength has now undergirded hundreds of widows and fatherless children, giving them hope for their future and joy in their present.

We have an obligation to our children to help them be the kind of people who not only get back up but also keep moving forward.

Every time.

Questions

1. Do you tend to shelter your kids or do you allow them to experience difficult situations?

2. How can your responses to your children's adverse situations positively or negatively influence their resilience?

3. What do you think kids learn from experiencing pain or seeing injustice?

4. Do you believe that difficult situations usually produce valuable life lessons? Can you reflect on such a time in your own life?

Our Response
This one's for the moms

M Y HOPE IS THAT NONE of you will ever be forced to carry the burden of burying a child. It is truly a life-altering event wrought with emotional pain. However, grief is not what this lesson is about. It's about being a woman and understanding our role in the emotional health of our family. In those early hours after Aaron was killed, I realized I could succumb to my grief, or I could attempt to stay strong for my daughters and my husband. I understood that my reaction would determine how everyone in the family managed the upcoming days and weeks.

Like it or not, we're the family stabilizer. If mom ain't happy, ain't no one happy, right? (And all the men reading this are currently shouting a huge "Amen!") We carry the weight of the emotional world on our shoulders, and if we're not careful to hold the balance, our family could quite literally fall apart. It's a heavy responsibility, but we *must* recognize it, we *must* respect it, and we *must* own it.

How *we* respond to emotional situations *will* be the blueprint for how our kids—and quite often our husbands—will respond. I encourage you to respond wisely. You have a choice. Never forget that.

Figure out now what you're made of, and when hard times hit—and they will—you'll be prepared to lead well.

Questions

1. Have you ever experienced a life-altering event? If yes, how did you respond? If no, how do you think you would respond?

2. In what ways could your response positively or negatively affect your children?

3. What would your response teach them?

4. How could your response affect the future of your family?

Resilience

Bend. Don't break.

I'LL NEVER FORGET THE LOOK on Aaron's face when he got that call ordering him to return to California just before his wedding. But more importantly, I'll never forget watching in awe as his sense of shock and disappointment gracefully merged into acceptance and peace—all within a matter of moments. His ability to respect authority, maintain self-control, and effectively compartmentalize what he was being told was brilliant.

And I was proud.

"God grant me the serenity to accept the things I cannot change, the courage to change the things I can, and the wisdom to know the difference." ~ Reinhold Niebuhr

So much truth in so few words. Yes, Aaron made quite a few phone calls that day and the next trying to change the situation, but he quickly realized that God had a reason for the change of plans and he accepted the new plan.

When we teach our children to embrace and practice Niebuhr's concept, we set them up for a purpose-driven, disciplined, life-giving existence. They will offer so much to this world. They will move mountains when others say it can't be done. They will encourage the discouraged and lift the heads of the weary. They will be world changers.

Yes, the principle is that powerful.

Questions

1. Do your kids have meltdowns when things don't go their way?

2. How can you handle things differently to correct these behaviors?

3. How can we grow resilient kids who are able to adapt to setbacks rather than revolt against them?

Family Decisions
Who wears the pants?

I BELIEVE THAT SOMETIMES WE, as parents, experience confusion between *taking into account how our decisions will affect our children* and *allowing our children to affect our decisions.*

Of course, we love our children. Of course, we want what's best for them. But in the end, we *must* be the ones making the tough choices. I've actually heard stories about parents asking their young children to make decisions for the family in critical life situations. Can you imagine the unnecessary burden that child now carries? What if it all went wrong? Whose fault would it be? What if five years down the road someone in the family wasn't faring well? Would that child bear the pain of lying awake at night believing it could be his or her fault? That's just not fair to a child.

Children do not have the capability to calculate risks versus benefits. They have no life experience to base decisions on, and most importantly, they have an undeveloped prefrontal cortex. I know it's hard as parents to carry the weight of tough choices, but we have to be intentional about keeping that pressure off our children.

When we're forced to make decisions that truly have an adverse effect on our children, we need to be open with them about the decision and explain it on a level they will understand. It's important to let them know in tangible ways that we understand and respect their sacrifices. Don't just say you appreciate what they're dealing with. Prove it.

Here's an example from when Billy and I made the decision to move away from Tennessee during Aaron and Tara's high school years. We had spent months praying about the decision, and we had talked with Aaron and Tara about our choice. In advance of our move, Billy and I took a trip to Florida so we could find a suitable home. We landed on a two-story condominium near the water. Upstairs was the master suite and a second, very large bedroom with its own private bath. Downstairs was a third bedroom—with no private bath—that was actually listed as an office on the real estate documents. In order to honor our children and to give them something to be excited about, Billy and I took the office. We put our two girls in the master and Aaron in the other suite. It really wasn't a big deal to us, but it was huge to them. They had ample space to host friends, and most importantly, they had their own bathrooms for the first time in their lives.

I'm not insinuating that we should feel guilty about what we've chosen and search for ways to "make it up to our kids." I'm saying we should look for simple ways to say, "I get it. I see you. I hear you. And I love you."

Questions

1. Have you ever been in a situation like the one our family experienced when deciding to move from Tennessee to Florida?

2. If so, did you allow your children's feelings to alter your decision?

3. In retrospect, would you make the same choice again?

4. What safeguards can be put in place to make sure our kids don't see themselves as victims of our choices?

5. What's the difference between spoiling our children out of guilt over a decision and supporting our children with added "I get its"?

Be a Champion
It's their journey, not ours.

IN BIG ORANGE COUNTRY IF your kid wasn't a good athlete, they might as well forget about social status. That placed a lot of pressure on us parents. We wanted our kids to fit in, to have it easy, so we did everything possible to turn them into good athletes. In the rush of it all, many of us neglected asking our children if they had any interest whatsoever in those sporting activities. We thought we knew best.

I loved basketball, and basketball was a huge sport for girls in the Obion County school system. So, naturally, I had Tara playing at a very young age—Saturday morning Pee Wee League, Jr. Pro, traveling team, then on to middle school and finally high school teams. Since she was barely five foot tall by the time she reached ninth grade, she, of course, played point guard.

And she was good.

She could sink three-pointers like nobody's business. She hustled hard and constantly racked up stats for steals and even rebounds. She was lauded with multiple awards through the years, so I assumed she wanted to take it to the next level and play ball in college. As she was wrapping up her senior year of high school, I was all prepared to help her meet with the coach at Palm Beach Atlantic University. I had pressed her several times about setting up a meeting when she finally mustered the courage to drop the bomb, "I don't really want to play ball anymore. I want college to be fun."

My heart dropped as I realized that maybe playing basketball hadn't been as much fun for her as I thought.

It's especially important that, as our children grow, we pay close attention to the development of their unique skill sets and passions. Sometimes it's a difficult task to put away *our* desires and to champion *theirs*, but it's an important task. Life is hard enough without unnecessary pressures from parents. We need to step back and feel the unbridled satisfaction of simply being our children's greatest cheerleader.

Questions

1. How do you feel about the "let them try everything" approach in figuring out what your children might be good at?

2. Do you tend to push your children toward *your* passions or do you let them choose?

3. What are some practical ways we can help our children identify their passions or talents?

4. How were you parented? Were you encouraged to follow your dreams?

5. How did that transfer to your parenting style?

The Winner's Circle

So...everyone gets a trophy?

THE NEW PHASE OF THINKING that "everyone gets a trophy" is not doing our children any favors. Kids are no longer learning to strive for success and, in reality, are being taught to settle for mediocrity. Possibly even worse than those things, the "everyone gets a trophy" mentality could be influencing the unfolding of an entire generation of braggers versus doers. The entitlement mentality is stopping society, as we knew it growing up, dead in it tracks.

Being successful at anything requires a no-quit attitude, a level of integrity and honesty—with others and with ourselves—and a sense that we are capable of overcoming whatever's put before us. Have you considered how many marriages fail because parents overly pampered their children and never taught them the concept of fighting and/or striving for something worthwhile?

Kids don't magically develop a no-quit attitude when they turn eighteen. Humility and fortitude are *learned* (and taught by us) from infancy. Self-worth doesn't come from being handed a trophy; it comes from looking at yourself in the mirror and knowing you stayed in the fight to the very end and gave it everything you had, no matter the situation.

Take just a minute to think about the kid who actually tries hard to win. How dismissive and disheartening is it to disregard that kid's personal achievement and lump him or her in with the kid who gave no effort whatsoever? And aren't we also teaching *that* child—the one who actually strived for success—that effort has no reward in this new society? Entitlement gets us nowhere. Its weight on the "doers" in our culture cannot be underestimated. If we teach our kids to be "doers" and "endurers," we will *all* enjoy the benefits of a thriving, world-changing generation.

Questions

1. How can you tell when a person feels entitled?

2. Compare and contrast a life marked by humility versus one marked by an attitude of entitlement.

3. Do you agree that humility is learned? If so, how can you teach your kids to be humble?

4. Do you think our society promotes an attitude of humility or an attitude of entitlement?

5. Which of these attitudes do you see in your kids and in yourself?

Work Ethic
The training ground

W E NEED TO RAISE KIDS who believe they can do anything but in order to do that we must first train them to have a teachable heart. As parents, we are the ones, not school teachers or Sunday School teachers, responsible for developing attitudes of humbleness and appreciation in our children as well as strong work ethics. If we parent our children well, we will teach them that many situations in life serve as a training ground for some aspect of their destiny and that their dreams will not be handed to them on a silver platter.

We need to instill the concept that anything worth achieving requires learning first and, second, requires effort and hard work because nothing is a "given." Aaron researched exactly what he had to know and be able to do physically in order to become a Navy SEAL. He spent hundreds of hours training his body to run faster and swim better. He didn't expect to walk into the Navy recruiter's office and be told he was automatically a SEAL. He understood that, in order to achieve his dream, he had to put forth the effort and go through the process.

We need to teach our kids that they *will* fail from time to time. And we also must teach them that failure is never final. It's imperative that we counsel our children to take the bumps of life in stride and to learn from their mistakes—which, by the way, requires admitting they've made them (another lesson in humility). No one is perfect, and our children need to understand that.

Every skill must be learned. Even walking and talking do not come to our children without a great deal of effort. If your kids are anything like mine, they took a few spills before those pudgy little baby legs began obeying their commands.

Our kids need to have an unquenchable thirst to dream big, grow steadily, and search wildly for the meaning and lesson in every situation they encounter. This is the process of becoming.

Questions

1. What are some practical ways we can teach our children to have a healthy work ethic?

2. Do you know someone who refuses to learn a new skill? How does that affect the people around him or her? How does the refusal to learn hinder advancement?

3. What role do you play in producing teachable adults?

4. Do you struggle to allow your children to work hard in the home? Do you find yourself either finishing their chores or feeling guilty that you made them work in the first place?

5. How could this type of parenting inhibit personal growth?

Letting Go
Failure to launch

A LOT OF PARENTS STRUGGLE to let go of their children and allow them to gracefully advance into adulthood. I understand that struggle, but that wasn't the case for me. I was that mom who couldn't wait for each new stage of life. Getting them to high school meant they would soon be driving *themselves* to all those practices (don't judge me), sending them off to college meant marriage was nearer, marriage meant grandbabies would soon be on the way, and on and on it went through life.

I realize I have a "glass half full" mindset, so I'll try to be delicate here for those who have a harder time with this. But if I may, I'd like to be frank as well (with an attitude of love that cannot be adequately conveyed when you're unable to hear my voice).

How many critical advancements have never come about due to a parent's unyielding leash or unreasonable fear? Would someone have cured cancer by now had a mom not said, "I don't want you to go to college so far away from home?" Or what if all those parents, whose children answered the call to defend their country after 9/11, had said "No, you can't go. I won't allow it." Would we have captured Saddam Hussein? Would Osama bin Laden still be roaming free?

Only God knows what we hinder by our fear. Only God knows what could have been had we responded in faith knowing we raised our children right and trusted them with their own futures.

At some point we must let go…even if our knees are shaking as we do so.

Questions

1. Does your heart fill with excitement or fear at the thought of your child one day leaving the nest?

2. Do you perceive those feelings as healthy or unhealthy?

3. How do your feelings affect your child's attitude toward adulthood?

4. How can you encourage your child to understand that the future is never to be feared but rather embraced?

Filling a New Role
Be their light

WHEN THE TIME COMES TO release our prior role as caregiver and decision maker in our children's lives and allow them to be independent, we cannot fail at such a critical step. I've witnessed graceful and not so graceful transitions. The fact that our children have reached adulthood does not mean they no longer need us. They simply need us in different ways.

To be honest, I struggled with releasing my role as my children left the nest. Yes, I was elated that they were moving on to the next stage of life, but it was hard to allow them complete independence. I soon realized, however, that if I didn't want to run around with hurt feelings twenty-four hours a day, building walls rather than bridges, I had better figure this thing out and adjust accordingly.

What our children need from us at this stage is a cheerleader, not a coach. And to be very clear—cheerleaders aren't in the huddle.

Adulthood is the time for us parents to rest in the firm foundation we have poured—whether or not our children are living lives that please us. (And don't think my story is a bed of roses. I've experienced both sides of the coin.) The important things are to continually let our children know we love them and to offer support and open arms. If your child's life is a train wreck, please don't beat yourself over the head by trying to own it. Remember, this is your *child's* life now—filled with *his or her* choices, not yours. Counsel when you see an opening, but unless the issues are of a psychiatric, dangerous, or criminal nature, try your best to allow your child the privilege—and the growth-producing process—of figuring things out on his or her own.

Questions

1. Does the thought that your kids might not fully rely on you one day give you a feeling of sadness or a sense of accomplishment?

2. As a mother, how do you feel *your* role in your children's lives should shift at different phases of *their* lives?

3. Are you building a foundation of mutual trust with your child? If so, how?

4. Would your grown children have the liberty to tell you that they don't want to share something with you? What would your reaction be in such a case?

Celebrate Life
It's the little things.

CAN YOU *FATHOM* THE REGRET I would have if I had told Aaron—on that last night we were together on earth—that I really couldn't stay up and talk because I was just too tired?

You never know. You *just never know.*

Make sure you're present—in the moment—with your kids. Put the phone down. Stop answering emails for the few hours between work and their bedtime. The world won't stop revolving. I promise.

Celebrate everything. Never miss a chance to do something special because that's when you take pictures. That's when you make memories. That's when everyone's focused on each other rather than the pointless sidetrackers that constantly derail our best-made plans.

Bonnie brought home a good report card? Stop what you're doing and go get some ice cream. Katie lost a tooth? Make a big deal of it. Wrap that gnarly little thing up like a fancy Christmas gift before you slip it under her pillow. Stop for pizza after Russell's ball game. Throw the biggest, craziest birthday parties your budget allows. And remember, it's not about how much money you spend; it's about creating moments that let them know your heart is turned inside-out in love with them.

Remember to choose your family first. Always choose your family first. In most cases, your kids will only be in your home for about eighteen years. Make sure they leave the roost knowing they were, and are, loved. You can't imagine what a step up in life a household of love will give them.

And last but not least, listen to them. I know…you'd rather put a drill bit through your eye than listen to them attempt to tell you about their day when their words won't come and you've got four loads of laundry piled on the couch! Ahhhh, it makes my chest feel tight remembering those days. But listen anyway. You can't expect your kids to talk to you about the big things when you never took time to listen to them talk about the small things.

Questions

1. Do you take advantage of opportunities to celebrate your child? Give some examples.

2. Have you ever found yourself unnecessarily prioritizing tasks over family?

3. Do you regularly tell your children you love them?

4. How can telling your children what it is—specifically—you love about them enhance their self-perception?

5. Have you ever found yourself so buried in the business of your own life that you missed something significant in your child's? For instance, you didn't have time to talk at bedtime when they wanted to tell you about their day. Later you learned that they'd been picked on and really needed you or they got passed their first love note and wanted your advice about checking "yes" or "no." Take time to make a list of all the things you don't want to miss out on and share that list with your child.

When Danger Lurks
It's their world too.

A s I TRAVEL THE COUNTRY speaking to various groups about Aaron's story, I always explain the profound impact September 11, 2001, had on his heart. I'm keenly aware that so much time has passed since that horrible day that many in my audience were either children, babies, or not even born yet. I'm not sure how much of the account of that morning is taught in our schools today, but this next generation needs to know what happened.

Children need to understand who we are as a nation and how we got here. I'm often taken aback by how easily I've forgotten what it felt like to meet a family member at the arrival gate when a flight landed. Do you remember? We've lost *many* freedoms since that fateful morning… freedoms today's children will grow up never knowing. And that breaks my heart.

A couple years ago, I had the great honor of touring the National September 11 Memorial & Museum with a firefighter who had been trapped under the second tower when it collapsed. In nearly every room we toured, his eyes welled with tears—which often escaped and rolled down his cheeks—as he shared stories of friends who died moments after he'd communicated with them that morning. I tried my best to hold it together.

As we descended to the lower floor, my heart emptied. There before me was a 60-foot long inscription on a wall covered with tiles in every imaginable shade of blue—"No day shall erase you from the memory of time. ~ Virgil" Behind that wall is a repository holding approximately 8,000 pieces of unidentified human remains.

It is incumbent upon us, as parents, to tell our children the true stories of our nation's history.

"Our dead are never dead to us until we have forgotten them."
~ George Eliot

Questions

1. Do *you* think it's important for children to understand their nation's history? Why or why not?

2. Do you think that teaching America's history to our children could make them feel more like they are a part of something bigger than themselves?

3. Do you think it's wise to shelter your children from the reality of frightening world events?

4. How can you help your child become involved in bettering their community, their country, and even their world?

Freedom Is Not Free
Consider the cost

THROUGHOUT THE PAST FIFTEEN YEARS of the Global War on Terror, over fifty thousand of our nation's sons and daughters have returned home to America's shores wounded and forever changed. They are burned, disfigured, missing limbs, struggling with traumatic brain injuries, and fighting post-traumatic stress. Almost seven thousand of our best and brightest have come home in flag-draped coffins. The average age? 26-½ years old.

When it was Aaron Vaughn's time to fight, to take *his* place in history, he fought with all he had. He knew it could cost him his life, yet he chose to defend, protect, and preserve for his children what had been defended, protected, and preserved for him. And he entered the battle with eyes wide open.

Aaron never took for granted that he was blessed enough to have been born in the United States of America, where men are free, because we *taught him* to honor the sacrifices of those who had gone before us. He honored our history. He studied the cost and prayed that if he lost his life young, he would lose it fighting for his country—dying to preserve the dream.

I'm not insinuating that your children need to join the U.S. Armed Forces to play out their roles in society. I'm asking you to *teach them* to be engaged. As a child, Aaron hung on every word his father shared about the great battles, those epic moments of conquest in America's long, tireless, faith-filled past. (Our nation's history is rich with stories of overcoming in order to create, protect, and enhance the hope known as America.) Teaching our children the importance of being informed about—and taking part in—the course of their nation's history is a crucial role we cannot neglect. Some of us may be raising children with the potential to become future local, state, or national leaders but who never will because of a lack of exposure. How can our children aspire to what they've never been exposed to? It's imperative that we continue raising children who "get it," who understand how their individual freedom came to be, and who know and respect America's history.

The most disrespectful action we can ever take toward those who forged our freedom is to refuse to acknowledge their sacrifices. As a woman, every time I cast my ballot, I see the faces of Alice Cosu, Dora Lewis, and Alice Paul—all women who fought to give future women the right to vote. I remember what the privilege of voting cost them and many others. I acknowledge that those who willingly fought to attain it granted it to me with complete selflessness. When I notice an interracial couple walking down the street hand-in-hand, I see the faces of Rosa Parks, little Ruby Bridges, and Martin Luther King, Jr., and I remember the battles fought to bring us to the civilized, all-embracing people we are today. We must *never* take these advancements for granted. We need to pass the wonder and awe of America's achievements on to our children in such a way that they will be inspired to one day pass it on to theirs.

At times, Aaron expressed frustration with the current culture. To him, the vast majority of our citizens were completely disengaged from the reality that men and women were dying for their right to live self-absorbed lives of little value. However, any time Aaron found himself going down that road, he quickly turned his thoughts: "But hey, that's why I do what I do. So they'll have the liberty to be anything they choose to be, even if they choose to be idiots."

Aaron and others like him did not fight because they hated what was in front of them. They fought because they loved what was behind them—the American way of life and our rich history. They knew that America, with all her flawed citizens, all her faults, failures, and divisions, all her bumps and bruises, is still the greatest land on earth...the Shining City upon a Hill...the hope of all nations.

Many have asked me during the past five and a half years a question that stings my heart: "Was America worth it?" I tell you unabashedly that my answer is "Yes. America and the American way of life is absolutely worth it." Would I give you my son if given the choice? Of course not. But I know in my heart that freedom's flames are fanned by the last breath of every patriot who has ever laid his or her life on the line for this nation's glorious endurance.

Everywhere I look I see the reason Aaron Vaughn gave his life. He knew that a Representative Republic is the noblest form of government ever devised by man but he also knew that this Republic would need protection. Even if he knew the outcome, I know in my heart he would do it all again.

I've taken my personal story to many elementary and high schools across the country, as well as a few colleges, and I always end my presentation about Aaron's incredible life of sacrifice and service with the same four slides.

First—a picture of our two daughters, Tara and Ana. I explain how very close Aaron was to his sisters, especially Tara, who was only twenty-one months younger than him. I tell my audience how these two were best friends their entire lives and how they did everything together for almost twenty years. Then I make this simple statement: "These girls... they gave you their brother."

Second—a picture of Aaron's widow, Kimberly. "She gave you her husband...the one true love of her life. The one she waited for for thirty years and lost only five years after finding him."

Third—a picture of Aaron's children, Reagan and Chamberlyn.

Our little Reagan—That look still rips my heart out every time I see this picture.

Chamberlyn at an Operation 300 camp

"Reagan's father will never sit in the stands at one of his football games and cheer him on or coach him on the ride home. Chamberlyn will one day walk down the aisle, and her father's arm will not be there to hold. They will spend their entire lives without their father. Because… they gave you their daddy."

And finally—a picture of Aaron in Afghanistan. "Here's Aaron. He gave you everything he had."

I end with this simple statement: "I'm begging you to live lives worthy of such sacrifice. Live like the opportunities you have before you were paid for with someone's blood, with someone's tears, with someone's eternal heartache. Because they were. Freedom is *not* free."

At the end of those sessions, I often hear comments like this one: "I never thought about my freedom that way." Sometimes a parent will approach me and say, "It never dawned on me that I had a personal responsibility to teach my children to be good citizens, to be engaged in protecting our freedoms and prosperity as a nation."

Freedom is never more than one generation away from extinction. We didn't pass it on to our children in the bloodstream. The only way they can inherit the freedom we have known is if we fight for it, protect it, defend it, and then hand it to them with the well-thought lessons of how they in their lifetime must do the same. And if you and I don't do this, then you and I may well spend our sunset years telling our children and our children's children what it once was like in America when men were free.

~ Ronald Reagan, 1961

We must instill nobility, gratitude, and patriotism into the core of our children's social make-up. Everything is at stake when a nation that represents freedom grows a society of people who think maintaining it is someone else's problem.

May we all live lives worthy of the tremendous sacrifices made on our behalves and may we raise a generation of children who do the same.

Dear Lord,
Lest I continue my complacent way,
Help me to remember that somewhere, somehow out there
a man died for me today.
As long as there be war, I then must ask and answer
Am I worth dying for?
~Eleanor Roosevelt

In place of questions, I leave you instead with an appeal. At the end of Aaron's story and before this Study Guide started, I challenged you to teach your children about Aaron. Please do that. Share this book with your kids if they are old enough. Let them look at the pictures of Aaron and those that he loved. Tell them the stories that you read. And, above all, start a discussion with them about what it means to be an American, a patriot, and a world changer.

Acknowledgments

I'D LIKE TO THANK FIRST and foremost my husband, Billy, the love of my youth. You've stood firmly beside me through the worst imaginable arrows the world could assault us with. I thank God for you, for your strength, for your love, and for your friendship. You are my best friend.

Next, I want to thank my daughters, Tara and Ana. Your consistent love and deep patience with my grief process (while working through your own) has inspired me, pushed me forward, and kept me on my feet when I felt I couldn't continue. Tara, your courage to begin Operation 300 in addition to your incredible strength to lead worship throughout the darkest days of your life has radically enhanced my faith in God and strengthened my steps in a way I'll never adequately be able to convey. I have an unimaginable level of respect for you. Thank you for always pushing me to be a better version of myself. Ana, thank you for always finding a way to make me laugh and for helping me to never take myself too seriously.

To my mom...I could never have asked for a better mom. You've been a rock throughout my life and I feel so blessed to be your daughter.

To Kimberly, thank you for loving my boy the way you did and still do. And thank you for being a strong mom to your babies.

To Matt, thank you for the way you love Ana and your children, and thank you for bringing so much laughter into our family. To Adam, you are more than a son-in-law; you have become a son. Thank you for the way you love Tara and the girls, and thank you most of all for the way you love God and how you live out your faith before us all.

And to my grandchildren: Belle, Lyla, Reagan, Chamberlyn, Audrey, and Micah—you are sunshine. You are hope. You are treasures to Pappy's and my hurting hearts. We love you with everything in us.

To Pete Hegseth…thank you for offering me a brand new life after Aaron's death—a life filled with new purpose and meaning. So much love to all the old gang from the "Defend Freedom Tour": Jus-tin, Phil, Amber, Kate, Caroline, Bill, Hannah, Jason, Natalie, Heather, and Kevin…thank you for filling those years with so much laughter and so much fun. I am a better person for having known each of you.

A special thanks to my sweet friend Tracy Bowen who doggedly pushed me to put this work on paper and carefully trained me to organize my thoughts on the page. This would never have come to be without you.

And to Kara Starcher, my editor…you are astoundingly gifted and such a joy to work with. Thank you for your patience and tenacity to get everything just as it should be.

And finally, to the Author and Finisher of my faith…Jesus. You are everything.

Karen Vaughn

About the Author

KAREN VAUGHN IS THE MOTHER of fallen US Navy SEAL, Aaron Carson Vaughn (SEAL Team VI). On August 6, 2011, Aaron was killed in action in the Tangi River Valley of Afghanistan when a chopper (call sign Extortion 17) carrying thirty Americans was shot from the sky while rushing into battle. The day Aaron's life ended Karen's began again.

Over the past five years, Karen has emerged on the national scene as a powerful spokeswoman for not only our defenders still fighting on foreign soil and securing peace across the globe, but also as an advocate for a better, stronger, more resilient America.

Carrying on Aaron's legacy has brought this Gold Star mother through the halls of Congress, into a National Press Conference, onto multiple national television sets and dozens of radio programs. She's been featured on large stages across this country as a keynote speaker, including a guest speaker position during the opening night of the 2016 Republican National Convention.

Karen has been married to Billy Vaughn for thirty-seven years and still believes their greatest accomplishment on earth was rais-ing their three children: Aaron, Tara, and Ana.

CONTACT KAREN

To book Karen for
speaking events, visit

OfficialKarenVaughn. Com

OR E-MAIL

KarenVaughnInfo@Gmail.com

Made in the USA
Coppell, TX
03 April 2020